R403

C000147403

INLAND CRUISING

INLAND CRUISING

Tom Willis

Pelham Books
London

First published in Great Britain by
Pelham Books Ltd
27 Wrights Lane
Kensington
London W8 5TZ

Copyright © Tom Willis 1987

All rights reserved. No part of this publication
may be reproduced, stored in a retrieval system,
or transmitted, in any form or by any means,
electronic, mechanical, photocopying, recording
or otherwise, without the prior permission of
the copyright owner.

British Library Cataloguing in Publication Data

Willis, Tom
   Inland cruising
   1. Boats and boating — Great Britain
   2. Motorboats
   I. Title
797.1'25   GV835.3.G7

ISBN 0 7207 1749 3

Printed and bound in Great Britain at
The Bath Press, Avon

CONTENTS

A STORY OF NAVIGATIONS

Britain is an island, the Britons a seafaring people. But that well-worn saw is of little relevance to this book. These pages are devoted not to the memory of Drake, Raleigh and Cook, but to an altogether different breed of navigator – the navigation worker, the original navvy, who built our inland waterways.

Look at a map of Europe. Find the capital cities. You will see that every one of them is built on a river or on the coast. In the days before made roads and rail, when most of these cities were founded, water provided the logical transport medium, presenting a uniquely level surface across which tons of loaded barge could be driven using a minimum of power. Wherever a river cut its way through the heart of the countryside on the way to the sea, boats could be induced to forge their way upriver to take cargoes and people into the interior.

The Romans were the first people to exploit this useful truth when they settled in Britain. They used the Thames to reach London, and there laid the foundations of the great capital city. They travelled up the Ouse to found York, up the Severn to build Gloucester and Worcester. They cut Britain's first canal, the still-navigable Fossdyke, from Torksey on the River Trent to the River Witham upstream of the settlement that would become Lincoln.

It takes a peculiar sort of arrogance to want to remould natural features for one's own benefit. The Romans had that arrogance, and with their roads, harbours and canals were Britain's first civil engineers. After they left, the Britons learnt once again to live with geography, and it was not until the end of the Dark Ages in the fifteenth century that minds began to turn once again to ways of improving on nature. The process started not with canals, but with the dredging of existing rivers to allow free passage to working barges.

Waterways travel in those early years must have been fraught with uncertainty. Although water finds its own level, rivers do not; they run downhill over an uneven bed. This presents no difficulty in the lower reaches of great rivers, but their upper reaches and smaller watercourses

Relic of a bygone age:
a horse-drawn narrowboat
on the Ashby Canal.

can be a problem. In dry periods the boatman has to contend with shallows and rapids; in flood, perhaps, with a river in spate.

Ironically, the solution was provided by people with whom the boatmen immediately found themselves in conflict. Rivers were useful as a transport medium for freight carriers, but to the locals who lived along the banks they were most valuable as a source of fresh food and power. Mill owners and fishermen built weirs across the stream, effectively dividing the river up into a series of steps.

This was just what the boatmen wanted: a means of controlling the depth of water. Unfortunately their interests were rarely compatible with those of the weir owners. To travel from one 'step' to another meant opening up a section of the weir, waiting until the initial flood of water had reduced and then hauling the boat through the gap. Each opening of the weir, known as a flash, lost a great deal of water from the upstream side, and the owners were understandably reluctant to open up more than was absolutely necessary.

Being built for reasons other than navigation, the weirs often created shallows below them. If a boat ran aground the boatman would have to negotiate with the weir owner for a flash to raise the level downstream. The owners were in a strong bargaining position and they knew it, often charging exorbitantly for the service or even refusing to open up. This led to ill feeling, frustration and, not infrequently, fights.

In the time of the Romans there were perhaps 650 miles of waterways in England that were naturally navigable. By the beginning of the seventeenth century the total had grown to about 750 miles. Much of this growth was due to the provision of flash locks, which for all their drawbacks did render navigable rivers that had previously been impassable. But the total includes a very significant stretch of ship canal, less than 2 miles long, built in 1564/6 to connect Exeter with the estuary of the River Exe.

The Exeter Ship Canal contained the first pound locks seen in Britain. With two pairs of gates in quick succession, the pound lock overcame most of the problems of the flash. Each opening lost from the upstream side only a volume of water equivalent to the size of the lock chamber; and boatmen were no longer obliged, when making upstream, to force their way through a gap against a strong current – they were now able to wait for the levels to equalize before entering or leaving the chamber.

It was an Italian, the amazing Leonardo da Vinci, who invented the mitre-gate lock that eventually became the standard, but throughout England variations on the basic theme of the pound lock were developed. Some of the variations, such as the guillotine gates on the Rivers Nene and Great Ouse, are still in use today.

Telford's incomparable Pontcysyllte Aqueduct, carrying the Llangollen Canal over the Dee Valley in North Wales.

After locks had proved their worth, full canalization of rivers became a real, practical possibility and was taken up enthusiastically. In many cases commissioners were appointed to administer the new navigations, as these canalized rivers were called, and prevent a recurrence of the old conflicts of interest. By 1760 there were more than 1,300 miles of navigable waterway in England.

River traffic now grew enormously, slashing the costs of freight transport between supplier and customer. Initially, of course, these savings were confined to routes between riverside towns. Suppliers not blessed with their own local river looked jealously at the savings being made by competitors using water freight, and determined to grab a piece of the action.

It is generally held to have been the third Duke of Bridgewater who ushered in the great age of canal building. Although he was by no means the first canal developer, this Midlands mine owner, together with his agent John Gilbert and an engineer called James Brindley, started a fashion that was to continue for the better part of a century. In 1759 work began on Britain's first arterial canal, the Bridgewater.

Although the Bridgewater Canal had been conceived principally as a way of bringing coal from the Duke's mines at Worsley to his customers in Manchester, the opening of the first section in 1761 found industrialists and mine operators queuing up to use it. The Duke's colossal investment of £200,000, which included the cost of cutting almost 50 miles of underground canals into the mines, was repaid from tolls within three years.

This astonishing return on capital attracted the eighteenth-century entrepreneurs like a magnet and led to a mad scramble throughout industrial England and Wales to get canals built linking river with river, town with town, coast with coast. Now began the Golden Age of canal building. Gangs of navvies descended on towns and villages, carved great trenches in the landscape, laid towpaths, built bridges, tunnels and locks. Up, down and through hills the links were forged; valleys were crossed with a single span of iron trough like Telford's great Pontcysyllte aqueduct.

Although John Gilbert had had as much if not more to do with the design of the Bridgewater Canal, Brindley got most of the credit and became the country's premier canal engineer. He was a visionary who foresaw an integrated network of canals and river navigations, and he started the process of linking England's four great river navigations, the Thames, the Severn, the Trent and the Mersey.

After Brindley came three truly great engineers who between them were responsible for a large proportion of the eventual canal network: William Jessop (1745–1814), Thomas Telford (1757–1834) and John Rennie (1761–1821). By the time the railways were established in the 1840s, the 1,300 miles of navigable river in Britain had been developed into a network of waterways over 3,000 miles long, making it possible to move huge quantities of freight from one side of the country to the

OPPOSITE
ABOVE *Working barge on the still commercially-used River Trent.*

BELOW *Strictly pleasure – a hire boat entering a narrow lock.*

other more cheaply than ever before. It was this network, more perhaps than any other single influence, that allowed the Industrial Revolution to take hold. Before the coming of cost-effective transport, industrialists' markets had perforce been local ones; afterwards, the whole country was open to their products.

Sadly, the speed of the development of the waterways carried within it the seeds of the waterways' destruction. Because most of the great canals were planned and constructed separately, the developers were free to decide on their own gauge, and many opted for the 7-foot narrow gauge first used by Brindley: narrow canals were much cheaper to build and easier to keep fed with water.

The result was that, while certain of the mainline navigations such as Jessop's London–Braunston Grand Junction Canal (now part of the London–Birmingham Grand Union), and the coast-to-coast links of Whitworth's Leeds & Liverpool and Rennie's Kennet & Avon, were built to dimensions that would pass substantial barges, many of the valuable linking routes such as the Shropshire Union, the Trent & Mersey and the Thames & Severn were closed to all but narrowboats.

As the railways developed it became clear that they had two distinct advantages over the canals. The first was speed, the second size. Speed was perhaps the less important of these, and could be offset against the cheaper running costs of the canal boat; but the size restriction kept the maximum load for a pair of working narrowboats down to some 60 tons, as against the railways' potential of several hundred.

An inland waterways craft with a difference: the preserved Humber Keel Comrade.

Disastrous breach of the Llangollen Canal, one of the prettiest in Britain, when the hillside collapsed under it.

The coming of rail thus spelt the beginning of the end for many canal operators. Often built virtually alongside the canals they were to compete with – because rail engineers, too, were anxious to minimize gradients on their lines – the railways steadily poached more and more custom. Traffic on the canals fell off to uneconomic levels; with less money coming in, the owners were prepared to spend less on essential maintenance work, and one by one the waterways fell into disrepair. In some instances the rail companies even bought up canals and allowed them to deteriorate to kill off the competition for good. One by one they were abandoned, in some cases even built over.

A Royal Commission was set up in the early years of this century to study the question of whether there was a future for commercial waterway traffic. The Commission's twelve-volume report was published in 1911, and one of its most significant recommendations was that the Cross – the canals connecting the Thames, Severn, Trent and Mersey – be enlarged to take 100-ton traffic. Only if this were done, argued the report, could a viable waterway system be re-established.

Sadly, the recommendations were ignored, and the decline of the canals continued. From 31 million tons before the outbreak of the First World War, annual traffic dropped to 21 million by 1919, 13 million by 1938. It takes an Act of Parliament to close a waterway, but in the years during and after the Second World War our legislators seemed to be working overtime on dismantling the system. In 1948 most of the remaining network was nationalized and the British Transport Commission (BTC) took over.

Pleasure craft and commercial traffic sharing the Manchester Ship Canal.

The BTC was expected to concentrate its meagre resources on maintaining the waterways that would repay attention. Since the BTC was a freight operator as well as a canal owner, commercial considerations had to come first, so the next twenty years saw yet more canals abandoned or closed.

Although the canals had attracted a few pleasure boaters even in Victorian times, and hire craft had been available on some waterways since before the Second World War, the BTC never really considered the network's amenity value. In 1949 the Commission stated in an article in the house magazine *Lock & Quay* that they were 'anxious to encourage the interest in pleasure boating', although their reluctance to spend real money to achieve this became apparent later on: 'We are seeing what can be done without undue expense to improve the canals that require attention to make them serviceable.' In the event, very little was done.

The Inland Waterways Association was founded in 1946, a pressure group determined to halt the decline of the canals and re-open the closed ones for pleasure traffic. It was not until 1962, when the British Waterways Board (BWB) was formed to take over responsibility for the waterways from the BTC, that the value of the network to boaters was given official recognition. Gradually the realization dawned that canals were worth preserving, even restoring, even in cases where they were of no value to commercial traffic. A succession of reports on the future

Restoration of a narrow lock. Much of the labour is provided by volunteers.

of the waterways showed the BWB's increasing awareness of the possibilities. The programme of abandonments stopped, and in 1968 the Board's recommendations for a network of 'cruiseways' were taken up and given statutory recognition in the Transport Act of that year.

Despite the Act, change was a long time coming, and it was not until the early 1970s that the revitalization of the network started in earnest. It was hoped that the cruiseway programme would become partially self-financing as it developed and as businesses such as boatyards and hire fleets came on to the canals. But restoration of a closed canal is almost as expensive as building one in the first place, and in many cases the BWB simply did not have the funds for rebuilding. Progress has been painfully slow, and on some canals it has been up to canal societies and gangs of volunteers to provide money and unpaid labour.

For some routes the task seems all but impossible. To restore through-navigation on the Forth & Clyde coast-to-coast link in Scotland, for example, would require the removal of no fewer than thirty-two obstructions ranging from road bridges to sections that have been filled in and, in the phraseology of the age, redeveloped.

Nor is it only the canals that need attention. Although rivers rarely run dry and most do a passable job of keeping themselves clear, as navigations they suffer from neglect. One example is the Avon, which was one of the first rivers to be canalized in Britain and which became impassable to commercial traffic for part of its length in the latter half of the nineteenth century. A massive restoration programme on both the Upper and the Lower Avon had to be completed, including the building of several locks, before the great river could be cruised throughout its length.

The future of some of Britain's waterways has never been in doubt. Travel down the Aire & Calder in Yorkshire and you will see relatively large ships and huge trains of barges, known as Tom Puddings, carrying coal from collieries to power stations. The Manchester Ship Canal is also still used extensively by commercial traffic in its lower reaches, as is the Caledonian Canal that cuts through Scotland's Great Glen and permits fishing boats and smaller coasters to make their way from East Coast to West Coast without having to brave the storms of the aptly named Cape Wrath and the Pentland Firth.

LEFT *Even today one of the cheapest ways of getting coal to power stations – the great Tom Pudding compartment boats.*

RIGHT *Working steamer on the Leeds & Liverpool Canal.*

So we now have what amounts to two canal networks. The commercial system still works – in fact improvements and the high cost of road and rail transport have drawn some users back to water transport – while the hopelessly uncommercial narrow canals have been taken over by the pleasure boat; there are now more than 25,000 holders of BWB cruising licences, and many thousands of other boats on non-BWB canals.

But this amenity, which we have grown to appreciate fully only in the past thirty years or so, is a fragile flower that needs to be nurtured and sustained if it is to release its full fragrance. Many writers, from the great L.T.C. Rolt onwards, have expounded at length on the value of the waterways. This book does not seek to cover that vast subject; but it is intended to give you the knowledge with which to explore them.

2

A CHOICE OF CRUISING GROUNDS

Britain's network of waterways covers an area that stretches from the south of England to the Highlands of Scotland, and from East Anglia's Broadland to the mountains of Wales. Not all are man-made; not all are 'ways' in the sense that they provide a route from one place to another — some, like Windermere and Loch Lomond, are lakes, locked in by fells or mountains and yet providing a pleasant cruising ground in their own right. (Purists might argue that the canals, or the canals and rivers, are the only true inland waterways, but for the purposes of this book we will take a wider definition that includes anywhere away from the coast where you can go boating.)

As might be expected of a 3,000-mile network, the variety is one of its chief attractions. Some of the canals are placid, river-like ribbons meandering gently through pretty countryside, following the curves and contours of the land. Others wind through cities and towns, offering a glimpse of a side of those cities that most visitors never see. Still others cut across the land, past, through and even under centres of industry, arrow-straight and flat in defiance of all topographical features.

Many canals offer a mixture of the rural and the urban, the scenic and the desolate. But it is not just lovers of nature or fans of Industrial Revolution architecture that are attracted to our waterways; it is anyone who wants an occasional opportunity to step off the helter-skelter world. Waterways are not hurryways.

Within the British inland waterways system there are several distinctly different types of cruising ground. They can be loosely grouped into five classifications.

THE NARROW CANALS

Much of the central network of canals in England and Wales is of narrow gauge. This does not necessarily mean that the canals themselves are narrow, but that the locks through which any boat must

*Under the motorway on the
narrow-gauge Birmingham
Canal Navigations network.*

pass were built to a standard 7-foot beam. These are the home of the
traditional narrowboat, a purpose-built craft usually in steel with a box-
like superstructure that makes the best use of the available space.
Incidentally, calling a narrowboat a barge in the presence of its owner is
the best method of making enemies on the waterways.

It was the narrow canals that first surrendered their freight to the
railways in the nineteenth century and even the wide-ranging and
optimistic proposals of the Royal Commission of 1911 never viewed
them as being commercially viable. Under the 1968 Transport Act,
which took away the former right of navigation on canals, some of
them were designated 'remainder waterways'. This effectively relieved
the British Waterways Board of any obligation to keep those canals
open.

Fortunately for us, several of the remaindered waterways have in
recent years been upgraded to 'cruiseway' status and are steadily being
restored. For this we can thank the Inland Waterways Association and
dozens of individual canal societies. Between them they have bullied
and cajoled local authorities and the BWB itself into supporting
restoration work, and have provided thousands of volunteers ready to
give their time and labour free to help with clearing and rebuilding.

The extra mileage of cruiseways has caused headaches for the BWB,
which has to maintain almost 60 per cent of the country's inland

waterways system out of a very straitened budget. A substantial backlog of work has built up, and stoppages – where navigation can be held up for months while repairs are carried out – are common, especially during the winter.

THE WIDE CANALS

Less standardized are the wide canals, a category that includes most of the commercial waterways in the country still in use. Those frequented by pleasure craft range from the Caledonian Canal, which will pass small coasters up to 150 feet long × 35 feet beam, to the Leeds & Liverpool, which although built to 14-foot gauge was given 62-foot-long locks; it was therefore impassable by standard-length (70-foot) narrowboats and gave rise to an individual design of working vessel called the short boat.

These two coast-to-coast routes are still open throughout their lengths. Sadly, not all the wide canals are. The most notable is the Kennet & Avon, once another east–west through route that linked the Thames with the Bristol Avon. This is gradually being restored but is still a year or two away from re-opening to through traffic. Another great artery, the London–Birmingham Grand Union Canal, was blocked for more than three years when the roof of Blisworth Tunnel collapsed and was only reopened in 1984.

Rural tranquillity: the coast-to-coast, trans-Pennine Leeds & Liverpool Canal.

George Orwell's little joke:
Wigan Pier, on a branch of
the Leeds & Liverpool Canal.

The fact that some of the wide canals are used commercially does not necessarily detract from their attractiveness. Some may pass great centres of heavy industry and power stations that still get their coal delivered by water, but then turn a corner into open countryside and dramatic rural vistas. Very few are not worth exploring.

Not all wide canals were built for commercial traffic. In Fenland are two sets of navigable waterways that carry the uninspiring title of drains. These were built principally to remove the water of the flat marshland, but also provide peaceful, remote navigations with unusual habitats and their own individual characters.

RIVER NAVIGATIONS

The early canal builders hoped to create a network of waterways that spanned the country. But they did not start with a clean sheet: a large part of the network had already been built by nature, with a little helping hand from man.

The first navigations were rivers, tamed with flash locks and weirs and ultimately pound locks. By dividing sometimes fast-flowing rivers up into steps the engineers were able to reduce current, overcome rapids and control the water levels so that floods and droughts were prevented.

A triumph of restoration: the Upper Avon, at Bidford.

Creating river navigations was easy compared with cutting new canals across virgin territory. With a virtually guaranteed water supply and in many cases an existing system of rudimentary locks and weirs, the engineers were able to build sizeable lock chambers. The Thames will pass boats of up to 109 feet long × 14 feet wide all the way to Lechlade, and larger craft further down; the Severn is open to Stourport for boats of up to 89 feet × 19 feet; even the River Nene will take 78-foot-×-13-foot craft as far up as Northampton. The size of the locks and the fact that there was no problem with water supply ensured that these rivers remained viable for commercial users long after the narrow canals fell into disuse; now, although much of the commercial traffic on some of these rivers has gone, it has been replaced by fleets of pleasure boats, guaranteeing their survival as navigable waterways.

Some of the rivers in the network, like the Wey or the Cam, are as well-mannered and placid as canals; others, such as the Trent and the Severn in their lower reaches, are volatile stretches of water quite unsuitable for inexperienced crews on small craft. Many of them, because the size restrictions of the canal network do not apply, are home to surprisingly large boats that live at the bottom of someone's garden and are used for both river and offshore cruising: regular weekends on the river, and one or two runs a year down to the coast or even overseas.

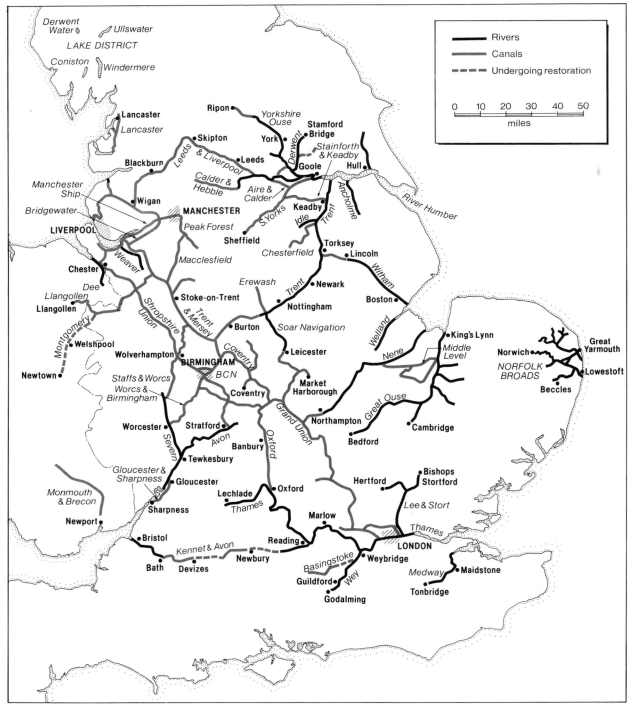

Inland waterways of England and Wales.

The most popular inland boating area in Britain, the Broads. This is Oulton Broad.

THE BROADS

A very large proportion of boating enthusiasts get their first taste of cruising in a small area of East Anglia. The Broads are a chain of shallow lakes formed centuries ago from drowned peat workings and linked by five rivers, the Yare, the Waveney, the Bure, the Thurne and the Ant. Well over 100 miles in overall length and with no locks, they have provided cruising holidays for countless millions of people for more than a century.

Because the rivers are tidal and run across relatively flat land bordered by the North Sea, the Broads can produce some challenging weather conditions at times. Nevertheless, they are an ideal training ground, with a plethora of boatyards and other boats always around to help you should you get into trouble.

With such a thriving market on its doorstep, Broadland is the home of many of Britain's best-known cruiser manufacturers, and the beamy (wide) craft they produce are popular not only on the Broads but also on rivers, lakes and some wide canals.

LAKES

Apart from the Broads, there are only a few navigable lakes in the UK. Windermere in the Lake District and Loch Lomond in Scotland are large but land-locked, so you have either to trail your boat there or charter one. Three of Scotland's other lochs – Ness, Oich and Lochy – are more accessible, being linked by the Caledonian Canal, while in Northern Ireland the River Bann gives access to Lough Neagh and the River Erne to the two loughs which share its name. Hire fleets operate on all of these.

That is more or less the extent of your choice for lake cruising, although motor boats are allowed on three other lakes in the Lake District (Ullswater, Derwentwater and Coniston) provided they keep to a maximum of 10mph – which is enough to cruise the length of Ullswater, the longest, in an hour. If you want to try them out you will have to be prepared to trail your own boat, as there are no hire fleets on any of the three and no access by water.

LICENCES AND PERMISSION

As history has shown, it costs money and effort to keep our inland waterways open, and, while some of this money comes from central government, boat users are expected to contribute their share. How much they have to stump up depends on who owns the navigation rights.

Most of the canals open to pleasure traffic are owned by the British Waterways Board (see the list on page 26). Any privately owned pleasure craft using or moored on these canals, whether powered or unpowered, has to have a valid Pleasure Boat Licence issued by the BWB. These are available for periods of one, three, six or twelve

LEFT *The freeze is on its way: last cruise before ice makes the canal impassable.*

RIGHT *Napton Locks, on the lovely Oxford Canal.*

From commercial port to marina: historic Gloucester Docks.

months; they are valid for the whole BWB canal network except Scotland, and permit the holder to use any of the facilities provided by the BWB, including water and locks, at no extra charge. They do not permit the owner to hire his or her boat out; hire boats have to have a special licence issued only after certain criteria have been satisfied.

In Scotland permission to use the waterways managed by the BWB is obtainable from the Board's Glasgow office, the address of which is given in the Appendix at the end of this book.

The BWB also owns a number of river navigations, also listed on page 26. Any boat with a valid Pleasure Boat Licence is entitled to use these, but for those who do not want to go to the expense of obtaining such a licence the Board also issues River Registration Certificates permitting them to use their boats on the river navigations only.

Certain canals are not in BWB hands, and except where reciprocal arrangements apply – such as in the case of the Bridgewater Canal – anyone wishing to use these has to get a licence from the managing authority. The same applies to river navigations outside the Board's control. Although most are owned by water authorities, navigation rights on some are in private hands; the Upper Avon Navigation Trust, for example, which was responsible for restoring the navigation above Evesham, can and does charge for use of the facilities it has installed there. The same goes for the Lower Avon.

Although you can moor overnight almost anywhere on the system provided it is safe and there is no indication to the contrary, permanent moorings are available in certain specific locations only. On BWB waterways many of these sites are controlled by the Board, whose local offices will issue a Mooring Permit if space is available, but there are also a number of privately owned or controlled marinas or stretches of bank where long-term berths are obtainable at rates ranging from modest to exorbitant.

Smaller boats that can be trailed behind a car may be launched from slipways throughout the system. These are owned variously by the BWB, navigation management boards, councils, boatyards or other private companies, and a fee of a few pounds is usually levied for each launch and recovery. Sometimes the owner will be expected to launch his own craft, in other places the slipway operator will do it for him A list of slips appears in Chapter 11, together with more advice on trailing.

INLAND WATERWAYS – WHO'S RESPONSIBLE

Aire & Calder Navigation: BWB

Ashby Canal: BWB

Ashton Canal: BWB

River Avon (Bristol): BWB

River Avon (Warwickshire): Stratford–Evesham – Upper Avon Navigation Trust; Evesham–Tewkesbury – Lower Avon Navigation Trust

Basingstoke Canal: Byfleet–Aldershot – Surrey County Council; Aldershot–Odiham – Hampshire County Council

Birmingham Canal Navigations: BWB

Bridgewater Canal: Manchester Ship Canal Co.

The Broads: Great Yarmouth Port & Haven Commissioners

Caledonian Canal: BWB (Scotland)

Calder & Hebble Navigation: BWB

River Cam: Great Ouse–Bottisham Lock – Anglian Water Authority; above Bottisham Lock – Conservators of River Cam

Chesterfield Canal: BWB

Coventry Canal: BWB

River Derwent: Yorkshire Water Authority

Erewash Canal: BWB

Forth & Clyde and Unions: BWB (Scotland)

Fossdyke Navigation: BWB

Gloucester & Sharpness: BWB

Grand Union Canal: BWB

Grand Union (Leics) & River Soar: BWB

River Great Ouse: Anglian Water Authority

Huddersfield Canal: BWB

Kennet & Avon Canal: BWB

Lancaster Canal: BWB

Rivers Lee & Stort: BWB

Leeds & Liverpool Canal: BWB

Llangollen Canal (Welsh): BWB

Macclesfield Canal: BWB

Manchester Ship Canal: Manchester Ship Canal Co.

Middle Level Navigation: Middle Level Commissioners

Monmouthshire & Brecon Canal: BWB

River Nene: Anglian Water Authority

River Ouse (Yorks): Trent Falls–Goole – Associated British Ports; Goole–Widdington Ings – Ouse & Foss Navigation Trustees; Widdington Ings–Swale Nab – Linton Lock Commissioners

Oxford Canal: BWB

Peak Forest Canal: BWB

Pocklington Canal: BWB

Regent's Canal: BWB

Rochdale Canal: Rochdale Canal Co.

River Severn: BWB

Sheffield & South Yorks Canal: BWB

Shropshire Union Canal: BWB

Staffs & Worcs Canal: BWB

Stourbridge Canal: BWB

Stratford-upon-Avon Canal: King's Norton–Lapworth – BWB; Lapworth–Stratford – National Trust

River Thames: above Teddington – Thames Water Authority; below Teddington – Port of London Authority

River Trent: Trent Falls–Gainsborough – Associated British Ports; Gainsborough–Derwent Mouth – BWB

Trent & Mersey Canal: BWB

River Ure: BWB

River Weaver: BWB

River Wey: National Trust

Lake Windermere: South Lakeland District Council

River Witham: BWB

Witham Navigable Drains: Witham Fourth District Internal Drainage Board

Worcester & Birmingham Canal: BWB

3

BOATS FOR THE WATERWAYS

In keeping with the variety of conditions to be found on Britain's inland waterways, boats for use on the system come in a number of forms. Although often treated with some derision by the coastal cruising crowd, it is very much a matter of horses for courses.

At one extreme, canal craft are not generally seaworthy – they do not have to be; they are not fast – again, they do not have to be; but they do have a couple of distinct advantages over the coastal or offshore cruising boat. The traditional narrowboat has astonishing accommodation for its size, thanks to a design that is the closest to a rectangular box that any naval architect has yet come up with. Canal boats are surprisingly economical; after all, their forebears had to be dragged fully laden from one end of the system to another by a single draught horse, and for most modern craft 10–20hp is more than adequate to push the hull along at the maximum permitted speed.

At the other end of the scale, the boats that ply the bigger rivers such as the Thames, the Severn, the Trent and the Ouse are often craft equally at home on river and sea. Although the riverboat may be underpowered compared with its seagoing equivalent – and logically so, because running a high-powered engine at low revs for hour after hour may damage it – the hull and accommodation will often be identical.

Almost all inland waterways boats have what is called a displacement hull. Perhaps the easiest way of explaining this is to say that it is the opposite of a planing hull, which at high speeds lifts itself bodily out of the water and skims along the surface. The displacement hull, on the other hand, remains firmly lodged in the water, displacing its own weight of water in accordance with Archimedes' principle (see Figure 3.1, overleaf).

In a car, the more powerful the engine, the faster you can go. It might seem that the speed a boat will achieve will depend on the power output of the engine or engines installed. This is true, but in the case of displacement hulls only up to a point. A displacement hull is subject to a maximum economical hull speed that is a direct function of its waterline length.

Figure 3.1 *Displacement hulls. Archimedes' principle states that a body immersed in a liquid displaces a weight of that liquid equivalent to its own weight. In other words, the amount of water represented by the shaded part of the hull in the left-hand diagram would weigh exactly the same as the boat. The water provides buoyancy that counteracts, pound for pound, the weight of the boat.*

With displacement hulls this principle is retained. There is no extra lift or buoyancy derived from the boat's speed, as there is with a faster planing hull. The boat sits squarely in the water, and as it moves along it pushes up a series of bow waves. The length of the bow wave will depend on the boat's speed, and as speed increases the crest will move further and further aft. When the distance between crests is equivalent to the length of the hull, the boat is travelling at its maximum hull speed. If it were to go any faster (right-hand diagram) the crest of the wave at the transom would drop astern of the boat; the stern would settle in the water and it would require a massive increase in power to overcome this and raise the speed further.

The maximum hull speed of any displacement boat is thus a function of its length on the waterline. It can be calculated by the formula $V = 1.4 \sqrt{L}$ where V = speed in knots and L = waterline length in feet.

This maximum can be calculated roughly by the equation $V = 1.4 \times \sqrt{L}$ where V denotes speed in knots and L is waterline length in feet (1 knot is 1.15mph). Thus a displacement boat with a waterline length of 25 feet will have a maximum hull speed of $1.4 \times \sqrt{25} = 1.4 \times 5 = 7$ knots, or 8mph. Once that speed is reached, however much extra power you add to the package your speed will remain more or less the same. Only by lifting the hull out of the water – in other words, by getting it to plane – could you increase speed significantly.

The other two popular forms of hull are the semi-displacement and the planing hull. With a planing hull there is theoretically no limit to the speeds that can be attained – the world water speed record now stands at over 300mph – although the faster you go, the more vulnerable the boat becomes and safety considerations put a practical limit on the maximum.

Semi-displacement – often called semi-planing – craft offer something of the best of both worlds. They are potentially faster than displacement boats of a similar size because their hulls are designed to give some lift at speed; at the same time, the fact that they remain well entrenched in the water gives them much superior seakeeping compared with the planing boat.

Displacement hulls may be slow, but they can still reach the maximum permitted speeds on canals and rivers and are therefore the natural choice for inland waterways. There are, however, some river cruisers that operate in both modes, with a planing hull that only comes into its own as they reach the coast and pour on the power. With such craft it is often a good idea to have a lower-powered auxiliary engine for use on the waterways so that you are not constantly running the engine at below its economical running speed.

THE NARROWBOAT

As has already been explained, the locks of the narrow canals were built to a standard width of 7 feet and a minimum length of 70 feet. Masters of economy, the Georgians and Victorians in turn built the largest possible craft that would fit into these locks, with the result that the 70-foot-×-6-foot-10-inch, 30-ton narrowboat became an industry standard.

The boatmen who operated these craft, and usually lived on board them with their families, found life anything but spacious. They lived, cooked, ate and slept in a small boatman's cabin, 6 feet 6 inches wide by perhaps 7 feet long, at the aft end of the boat. From the front of the cabin to the bows was clear hold space capable of taking 30 tons of cargo.

As engines became more common, narrowboats were worked in pairs, the powered boat (called the 'motor') towing an unpowered 'butty'. The engines carried with them a weight and space penalty, limiting the motor's payload to 25 tons. On the wide canals, such as the Grand Union, both motor and butty could lock through together, but on the narrow canals – except where two locks were built side by side – they would lock through one after the other.

Throughout the commercial life of the narrow canals the 70-foot narrowboat retained its supremacy. Only specialist craft, such as the icebreakers used to clear a way through the frozen waterways in winter, were built to more modest dimensions.

When the first canal trippers came on to the waterways there were thousands of superannuated motors and butties that could be picked up for the proverbial song and converted, with the result that the narrowboat took on a new lease of life. Designed to offer maximum cargo-carrying capacity and economy, it was the ideal boat also for the leisure canaller. It still is, and though many owners are now opting for 40- or even 20-footers, these are simply truncated versions of the original.

The standard narrowboat nowadays has a robust steel hull, almost slab-sided though with substantial rubbing strakes to protect the hull in locks, and a box-like superstructure high enough to provide standing headroom throughout yet low enough to allow the helmsman, who steers from the aft deck, to see over the coachroof. Because the superstructure uses virtually the full available beam, leaving a very narrow and somewhat precarious side deck, anyone wanting to get from one end of the boat to the other has either to crawl over the coachroof or walk through the cabin. It is therefore important that the accommodation is laid out to provide a clear passage.

Figure 3.2. *Two sizes of narrowboat: a 2/4-berth 28-footer (left) – the settee and table convert to a double – and an 8/12-berth 65-footer with eight fixed bunks and two convertible dinettes. Note how all the furniture has to be laid out either side of the accommodation to give a clear passageway through the boat from bow to stern.*

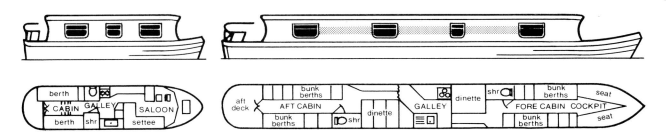

Accommodation layouts vary from builder to builder, although the constraints imposed by the narrow beam and the need for a through-route limit the number of options to some extent. Typical layouts for a 28-footer and a 65-footer are shown in Figure 3.2.

Narrowboats are invariably powered by an inboard engine, usually diesel, which drives a slow-turning propeller via a single in-line shaft. They are steered by means of a tiller that operates a large rudder immediately aft of the prop. The length of boat ahead of this rudder makes for special handling techniques, which are dealt with in Chapter 6.

There were many different varieties of craft used by the working boatmen of the eighteenth and nineteenth centuries. They were usually built to the maximum dimensions of the canals on which they travelled; thus the Leeds & Liverpool Canal, built to 14-foot gauge but with locks only 62 feet long, gave rise to the wide-beamed 'short boat'. Few of these survive today, and although they offer much greater scope for imaginative conversion than narrowboats, they are of no use to the pleasure boater who wants to explore the whole system.

NARROW-BEAM CRUISERS

Aside from the narrowboat proper, there are many other designs of cruiser suitable for use on the narrow network. Any boat with a beam of less than the magic 7 feet will do, but as these are usually scaled-down versions of conventional river cruisers it is rare to find one longer than about 24 feet.

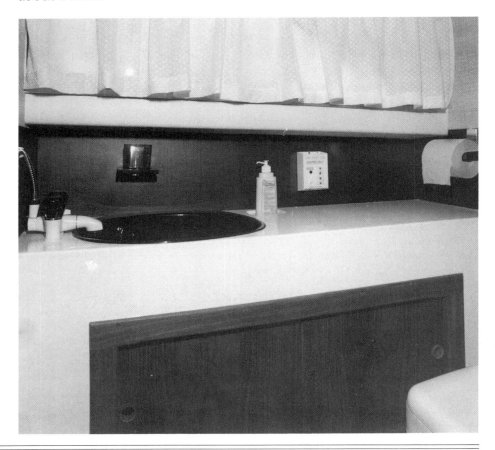

Storage space is at a premium on boats. This hire-boat toilet compartment offers plenty of surface storage, but could do with more lockers.

Narrow-beam cruisers are usually built in glassfibre; some smaller, older craft are of plywood. Plywood, although light, can be easily damaged and so is much more vulnerable to the rough treatment that boats tend to get in locks.

One slightly irritating foible common to both boat builders and hire operators is a tendency to be optimistic about the number of people a boat will sleep. Narrow-beam cruisers, because they are neither as long nor as rectangular as the classic narrowboat, invariably have less-than-generous accommodation, and it pays to treat the brochure's claims with caution.

Most builders will try to cram in as many berths as possible, at the expense of gangways and stowage space. This will usually mean that bunks double up for day use as seats or dinettes, and have to be made up each night and put away each morning. While this might be acceptable for a weekend, it leaves little room to stow more than a toothbrush and certainly no space for any of the usual impedimenta that accompanies the average family on holiday.

Narrow-beam cruisers may be powered by inboard engines, either petrol or diesel, or outboards. The inboards will drive through conventional shafts, a hydraulic drive unit (rare) or an outdrive leg (see Chapter 4). Surprisingly little power is required, as these craft are both lighter and more hydrodynamic than narrowboats, and it is once again important not to install more power than necessary or you will both waste fuel and risk damaging your engine.

RIVER CRUISERS

On rivers the problems of water supply that beset the canal builders do not apply, so all river navigations are built to wide gauge. Cruisers designed for use on river and wide canal can therefore be built as beamy as required – the length/beam ratio may be as low as 2.5:1 – and accommodation is generally much more spacious than that found on a narrowboat or narrow-beam cruiser. However, the comments about sleeping accommodation made in the last section still apply, with most designs opting for dual-purpose living/sleeping areas. Figure 3.3 shows typical layouts for a 27-footer and a 40-footer.

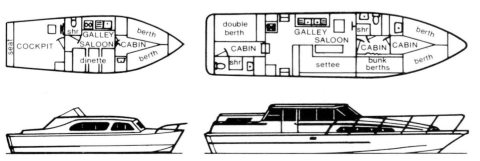

Figure 3.3. *Two sizes of river cruiser: a 2/4-berth 27-footer (left), with a small cockpit and outside helm, and a 6/8-berth 40-footer. Although the helm position is inside, the saloon has a wide sunroof that can be pulled back to give open-top cruising. On some boats the whole roof slides back to turn the entire saloon into an open centre cockpit.*

River cruisers may be required to plug upstream against a strong current, so they will need more power than a comparable canal boat. Inboard petrol or diesel engines and outboard petrol engines are the preferred power units, inboards driving through conventional shaft or outdrive leg, and sometimes on larger craft a twin installation is chosen for added safety and improved manoeuvrability.

TRAILER BOATS

Up till now consideration has been given mainly to larger boats that are kept afloat throughout the season, and in some cases throughout the year, because of the sheer impracticality of lifting them into and out of the water every time their owners want to use them. Yet given a large enough car and a small enough boat, launching and recovering the boat every time it is used becomes a worthwhile option, providing the opportunity to sample the whole waterways network – see Chapter 11.

MATERIALS

The old commercial inland waterways craft were built of wood or steel, and the latter remains the preferred material for modern narrowboats. Its strength allows even the most cack-handed beginner to take a boat into a lock without risk of major damage; and although it needs to be painted regularly to protect it from corrosion, this will often be necessary anyway to obliterate the evidence of intimate encounters with a lock chamber. A steel boat is usually built up from a framework of ribs to which steel plates are fastened, with rubbing strakes of D-section steel welded on to protect the plating. The end product will be heavy but immensely strong.

Cruisers, on the other hand, are generally built in glassfibre-reinforced plastic, known for short as GRP or just plain glassfibre. Sheets of glassfibre matting are laid inside a female mould and impregnated with a polyester resin, then covered with another layer of matting. This is impregnated in turn, and so on. When all the layers, or laminations, have been applied, the resin is allowed to 'cure', binding the laminations together to produce a single hull moulding. This can then be lifted out of the mould and fitted with bulkheads, engines, floors and so on before fixing the deck assembly – usually another glassfibre moulding – in place.

The result is a relatively strong boat, much lighter and cheaper than an equivalent steel craft. It will not be as strong as a steel boat, but when damaged is easier to repair, and small repairs can be undertaken by an amateur. Another advantage is that maintenance work is minimal. Although glassfibre can suffer from a damaging and expensive-to-remedy ailment called osmosis, this is not often a problem and is usually the result of poor manufacture rather than lack of maintenance.

Now very rare on new boats, plywood used to be common on smaller canal and river boats. Lighter and cheaper even than glassfibre, this material does have the drawback of needing constant attention if it is not to suffer from rot. It is also likely to come off worst in any collision with a more substantial boat or lock side, although again repairs can be carried out even by amateurs.

Older wooden boats will be built up around solid frames, with horizontal planks (or 'strakes') butting or overlapping each other or with two or three sheets of ply moulded around the frames before being glued and nailed into place. This produces a very good-looking hull of medium strength, but again regular maintenance is required to prevent the onset of rot.

ACCOMMODATION

There is no such thing as a typical layout for any cruiser, as the interior space available may vary from a thin oblong to something approximating a triangle or an ellipse. Berths may be dedicated or dual-purpose, serving both as bunks to sleep on and as seats to sit on; layouts may be open-plan or divided into separate cabins; helm positions may be enclosed or out in the open. There are, however, certain features common to most boats, and it is worth taking a brief look at these.

Convertible dinette, used to form an occasional berth.

Galleys

For many people the most important part of the boat, the part where food is prepared and cooked, is often poorly equipped, with a small stove and sink, perhaps a fridge, a few lockers and worktop space that could be outclassed by any decent-sized kitchen table ashore. Worktop space may be provided by the dinette, but if this is occupied when the cook starts to prepare the food someone will have to give way. Small wonder, then, that many boat chefs prefer to take the opportunity to eat ashore or to confine their cooking to packeted or tinned meals.

That having been said, the fact that cruising holidays often leave the normal cook with time on his or her hands allows a lot of scope for more creative culinary efforts if the inclination is there. More information on this is given in Chapter 7.

Water

Even if you do not cook aboard, you will need a constant supply of water for washing and drinking. All but the smallest craft will have a built-in water tank made of glassfibre, plastic or stainless steel. Stainless steel is expensive but best, as it does not impart any taste to the water. If your boat has a plastic tank it makes sense to drain the tank before leaving and refill every time you come aboard. There are also various proprietary brands of purification tablets available which prevent the growth of bacteria and take away any bad taste, as well as filters that can be plumbed into the supply pipe which do essentially the same job.

Water systems are either pressurized or fed by manual or electric pumps. Manually pumped systems will have either a foot pedal or a lever on the tap that, when operated, draws water up the pipe and into the sink; an electrically pumped system works on the same principle, except that turning on the tap/switch operates the pump motor to draw the water. Both these options have the minor disadvantage that the water comes in spurts with each pulse of the pump.

The pressurized system, on the other hand, has a conventional tap and a pump which senses the pressure in the outlet pipe. The pump operates automatically whenever the pressure in the system falls, so that there is a constant head of pressure against the tap. This ensures a steady stream of water when the tap is turned on. Again, though, there is a disadvantage in that pressure tends to leak out of the system even when the tap is off, so the pump is regularly switching itself on and off. If you do not want your night's sleep disturbed, you have to turn off the system at the main switch.

Where fitted, hot water systems are usually of the pressurized variety. There are several ways of getting a hot water supply: an Ascot-type instant gas heater, a full central heating system, or a heat exchanger. The last is the simplest and most common, deriving its heat from the engine cooling water, but it does have the drawback that hot water is available only while the engine is running or for a limited period afterwards.

OPPOSITE *Interior of a narrowboat – 7 feet is not very wide, especially when you have to include a passageway.*

In many boats, showers drain into a sump below the waterline. This means that the dirty water has to be pumped out of the boat, and a separate electric pump is usually fitted for this purpose. Some operate automatically, but others have to be switched on – and off again when the sump is empty, if you do not want a burnt-out pump.

Electricity

Separate generator sets are rare on inland waterways craft, although you can now buy fairly cheap small portables that will not disturb the neighbours every time you start them up. Nevertheless, a 12V or 24V DC electrical system derived from an engine-driven alternator will provide enough power for most needs. There may also be an alternative 240V AC ring, but this will be available only when the boat is moored and hooked up to a shore supply.

On any boat with accommodation at least two batteries or banks of batteries will be necessary, one to start the engine and the other to run the lights, fridge and other services. They should be wired up so that even if you drain the services bank, for example by over-use of lights, there will still be juice left in the other bank to start the engine.

Fluorescent lights are preferred for the accommodation, as they are much more economical than the bulb variety. There will usually be two other types of light aboard; a spotlight, essential for tunnel transits, and navigation lights. Most canal boats tend not to carry these, but they should if any night travel is likely, especially on rivers.

The colour and positioning of navigation lights is prescribed by the International Collision Regulations. On the port side showing from dead ahead to 22½ degrees abaft the beam there should be a red light, with a green light showing over the equivalent sector on the starboard side. There should also be a white light at the masthead, showing over the sector covered by the two sidelights, and a white stern light showing over the sector not covered by the sidelights.

The Collision Regulations were drawn up for ships at sea, and now include numerous exemptions for smaller craft: boats of under 7 metres (23 feet) in length and capable of no more than 7 knots need only show an all-round white light; boats of under 12 metres (39 feet 4 inches) may carry a combination masthead/sternlight (that is, an all-round white) in place of the two separate lights; and boats of under 20 metres (65 feet 7 inches) may combine the sidelights as a single bicolour mounted on the centreline. However, these exemptions do not apply on some waterways, such as the Thames; here the Thames Navigation and General Byelaws of 1957, which make no mention of combination lights, are still in force.

Toilets

For obvious reasons there are restrictions on the use of sea toilets (that is, ones that discharge the waste directly overboard) on inland

Baths are impractical on board, but most boats over about 25 feet have room for a shower.

waterways. All river and canal boats therefore have either chemical toilets which treat the waste and store it until it can be disposed of, or toilets that flush into a sealed holding tank which can be emptied at one of the pump-out stations thoughtfully provided throughout the network by the BWB and other managing authorities. Nearly all hire fleet operators have pump-out facilities, and often a reciprocal arrangement exists whereby they do not charge for emptying the tanks of other operators' hire boats.

LEFT *Where fixed lavatories are used on inland waterways craft, they usually feed into a holding tank.*

RIGHT *Portable toilet on a river cruiser. The base collects waste hygienically, and can be detached and taken ashore for emptying.*

Cookers

There is a wide variety of cookers available for use on boats, ranging from full-sized stoves of the type you have at home to tiny one- or two-burner hobs without either oven or grill. Electric cookers are rare because of the current required to run them – a cooker drawing 30A from a 240V mains would need an impractical 600A on a 12V supply. Traditional narrowboats may have solid-fuel or oil-fired stoves, but these too are uncommon.

Modern boats therefore tend to have cookers that run on bottled gas, either butane or (rarely) propane. This has to be treated with care; the gas is heavier than air, and any that leaks out will sink down into the bilges, building up over a period of time to present a real threat. The cylinder should be stored outside the accommodation if possible and be connected to the cooker by copper pipe. The supply should never be left on for longer than necessary, and should be turned off at the cylinder valve when the cooker or heater is not in use.

The basic principle of operation of a boat cooker is the same as that of a normal household one, but many first-time users are puzzled by a safety feature, found on most modern cookers, known as a 'flame failure device'. This is designed to shut off the gas supply to the ring if the flame is blown out by the wind or otherwise extinguished (for example, by milk boiling over). When the ring is in use, a thermocouple next to the ring is heated up by the flame and allows the gas valve to remain open; if the flame dies, the thermocouple cools down and closes the valve.

On first lighting the ring, therefore, the cook has to override the thermocouple to allow the gas through. This is done by keeping the main ring control knob depressed until the thermocouple has heated up enough to operate normally – normally twenty seconds is ample. If you simply turn the knob and try to light the ring, nothing will happen.

Smaller cookers are not plumbed in, but have an integral gas bottle of the Camping Gaz type. Although a cheaper type of installation, this is rather more expensive to run, and the special gas bottles are not quite as easy to obtain as the universal cylinder.

One drawback of the gas cooker is that the gas releases a large amount of water into the air as it burns – almost twice its own weight, in fact; 10 kilograms (22lb) of gas will produce 18 kilograms (40lb) of water vapour. Good ventilation is therefore essential.

Fridges

A means of refrigerating food to keep it fresh – and making ice for drinks – is almost as indispensable as the cooker itself. There are two forms of fridge in common use on boats, absorption and compressor types. Absorption fridges work, paradoxically, by heating up a solution of ammonia and distilled water and then allowing it to evaporate inside a sealed evaporator in the fridge, a process that draws heat from the food (cold, in physics, is defined as the absence of heat, and thus cooling always involves the removal of warmth rather than the injection of 'coolth'). They can be powered by either gas or electricity, and some models will run off both.

The second form of fridge uses the same principle of allowing a gas to evaporate inside the fridge, but in this case it is a compressor that heats up the refrigerant (if you pressurize a gas, its temperature rises). Most household fridges are compressor types.

Compressor fridges run on electricity only, and have two main disadvantages: they use a lot of current, and are generally noisy. Against this has to be set the fact that they will operate at almost any angle, because the compressor sucks the refrigerant back down from the evaporator. In contrast an absorption fridge, which has no pump and is therefore much quieter and more economical in operation, relies on gravity to circulate the refrigerant. This means that installations should be as near vertical as possible, but since inland waterways craft rarely roll or heel, it is not usually a problem.

Ironically, an absorption fridge's advantage of quiet operation can also be a disadvantage, particularly with gas-fired models. Having lit the heater, it may not be possible to tell whether the unit is working properly – unlike a compressor fridge, whose humming immediately confirms that all is well. One way of preventing the constant switching on and off of the compressor from disturbing your night's sleep, incidentally, is to keep a couple of cold packs in the fridge. These can be left in the icebox during the day, then placed in the main compartment at night, allowing you to switch the fridge off and still keep the food cool.

Heaters

British summers being as unpredictable as they are, even if you go boating only in the high season there is a case to be made for installing some form of space heating aboard. Ideally this should be independent of the engine so that the accommodation can be kept warm at night or when moored without the need to run a noisy diesel.

Traditional narrowboats may have a wood- or coal-burning stove aboard, but most modern craft that have heating will use gas, diesel or paraffin systems. The simplest option is a self-contained gas heater, preferably of the catalytic type, which is both safer and more economical than one that burns with a flame. One minor drawback of the catalytic heater is that the lack of any visible flame makes it difficult from any distance away to confirm that it is working, but a hand held in front will usually tell. It is also very important when installing and operating catalytic heaters to ensure that the cabin is well ventilated.

Diesel or paraffin heaters are usually sited outside the accommodation, with air ducted in through large-diameter pipes. They use very little fuel, typically a pint every couple of hours for a 1.5W heater.

Berths

Few boats have the space to be able to provide separate cabins for everyone, or even every couple, on board, and there will usually be occasional berths in the saloon or in the cockpit. The most popular type has foam cushion underneath, preferably at least 4 inches thick. Where the foam is not a single slab – such as on convertible dinette berths – there may be a hard fillet of wood in the gap, and extra cushioning

Classic V-berth arrangement in the forecabin of a river cruiser. By inserting an infill board and cushion in the space between, the berths can be converted into a triangular double.

might be necessary. Berths in the forecabin of river cruisers are often V-shaped, with an infill board that can be fitted between them to create a triangular double.

DECK EQUIPMENT

By and large, there are two types of deck equipment: fittings to prevent passengers falling overboard and fittings to keep the boat safely moored where you want it. In the first category, cruisers are generally better endowed than narrowboats, with pulpit, stanchions and guardrails forming a fence round the deck, and grabrails on the coachroof or sides of the superstructure which you can hang on to as you make your way along the side decks. But all these fittings make it more difficult to hop on and off the boat, so while they are essential on seagoing craft they may be more trouble than they are worth on canals and rivers.

Mooring equipment, however, is essential. Every boat should have a strong cleat, bollard or samson post on the foredeck and each quarter, and preferably one halfway along each side deck as well. Fairleads on the edge of the deck near each cleat will make your lines last longer and prevent them wearing holes in the boat.

Most of the time you will be tying up either to shoreside rings or bollards or to your own mooring stakes, but you should still carry an anchor or mudweight; if your engine fails, it may be the only way of stopping the boat from heading inexorably towards a weir. The anchor or mudweight, which may also come in useful if you go aground, should be kept permanently tied ('bent on' is the correct expression) to its own line, and stowed on or under the foredeck.

Anchors for inland waterways craft are seldom very large, so a windlass should not be necessary. A bow roller, which acts as a form of fairlead for the anchor cable as well as providing a means of dropping anchor without it hitting the hull, is a good idea.

Every boat should have a minimum of four mooring lines, each one at least the length of the boat. Nowadays these are likely to be made of artificial fibre, the favourite materials being nylon (which tends to stretch), polyester and polypropylene. For tying up where there are no bollards, rings or other convenient fixtures, you will also need a pair of mooring stakes (carry three, in case you lose one) and a club hammer. The stakes need not be anything more than steel rods, around 18 inches in length.

River cruisers should carry at least four good fenders, and preferably four per side (narrowboats tend not to use fenders, at least in locks – there is no room). Space should not be a problem, as most of the time they will be left dangling over the side; this habit is frowned upon by coastal water boaters, but is perfectly acceptable on inland waterways, where you moor up as many times in a day as the coastal cruisers do in a week.

BUYING A BOAT

Boating need not be an expensive hobby. By hiring you can take three week-long holidays a year and still spend less than you would on a fortnight in the sun. But sooner or later most enthusiasts find themselves hankering after their own boat. Ownership means freedom to take advantage of the occasional opportunity as it presents itself: a weekend when other plans fail to materialize and the whole family is unexpectedly free, a day in the middle of the week when you are not too busy at the office and the sun is blazing in a cloudless sky.

Owning your own boat also allows you flexibility in your cruising. There is no need for the frenzied dash back to the hire base that is the hirer's penalty for staying too long in the pretty reaches; you can simply leave the boat at a nearer, more convenient mooring and come back to collect it next weekend.

Finally, ownership gives you the right to exercise your own choice in how the boat is laid out, decorated and equipped. You don't like the pink curtains? Change them. You can do without the sixth bunk? Rip it out, and put in something useful like a locker instead. But don't try doing it on a hire boat.

Buying New

Apart from electronic equipment which seems to fall in price every year, nothing is as cheap as it used to be, and boats are no exception. A new boat with more than overnight accommodation will set you back a minimum of £10,000, while a good 30-foot river cruiser is likely to cost £1,000 a foot. Prices are governed by length but are not, of course, directly proportional. Some examples of 1986 prices of different boat types are given on page 48.

If you are buying new, it pays to have had experience of cruising in a variety of boats so that you know what you want. This is not just because of the risk of making an expensive mistake, but because one of the main advantages of buying new is flexibility of choice. Boats are not mass-produced, and even those builders who refer grandly to their 'production lines' will usually be prepared to alter or amend their standard layouts or specifications to suit your needs — provided you know what they are.

Boat shows are a good place to start looking, unless you want a traditional narrowboat. Get-togethers such as the Inland Waterways Association's annual rally also offer a chance to see a lot of boats at once, and most owners will be only too delighted to show you round their craft, tell you who built it and tell you frankly what they think of it.

You might find your ideal boat in the pages of a hire brochure, in which case it will be worth hiring one for a week to see whether it is as good as it seems. Magazines such as *Canal & Riverboat*, *Motor Boat & Yachting* and *Waterways World* all carry out regular boat tests and report their findings.

Once you have decided on a boat, approach the builder or his dealer and start negotiations. It may be possible to buy from stock, but as boats are expensive items to hold in inventory, more often than not yards will only build to order. You will be asked to sign a contract and pay a deposit, with other payments due at intervals as work progresses. A word of warning here: companies have been known to fail in the boat industry as in any other, and in a number of cases those customers who have had boats in building at the time of the collapse have seen their investment snapped up by the primary creditors.

The only way of avoiding this disaster is to ensure that title to the boat passes to you progressively with each payment you make. This means that even if the builder goes bankrupt you will be able to take what exists of your boat and have another yard complete the work. The British Marine Industries Federation, the trade association for the industry, has designed a contract that does the job, and it is worth asking the builder if your agreement with him can be based on the BMIF standard contract.

It is remarkable how many people will order boats costing more than a small house without taking the elementary precautions to protect their rights that are considered essential in house purchase. Do not sign the contract or hand over any money until you have consulted your solicitor: the consultation fee will be nothing compared with what you could lose if things go wrong.

Having agreed terms, signed the contract and paid your deposit, you then have to wait for your new boat to be completed. Do not wait in silence: remind the builder of your existence from time to time, especially as the contractual delivery date looms. If you don't, he may assume you will not be too worried if delivery is late and may be tempted to give priority to finishing off a boat for someone else who is more vociferous than you.

The final payment should be made on acceptance. Again, this is something that should be stipulated in the contract. Don't dream of handing over the money until you have had a trial run and until the builder has agreed to rectify any faults that you find.

Reading the above, you might be forgiven for thinking that boatbuilders appear to be an untrustworthy lot. Perish the thought. The vast majority of transactions will go through without upsets, but that is no consolation to the customers of yards who, sometimes through no fault of their own, fail to deliver the goods. Unless you can afford to lose the money you are spending on your boat, you have to protect yourself.

Buying Secondhand

Even if you can afford to buy a new boat, you might consider the alternative. Buying secondhand means that a tight budget can be stretched to get a bigger, better boat than you could afford with a new build; or that you can buy the same model and use the money saved to pay for extra useful equipment.

Used boats for sale are advertised in all the magazines listed previously, as well as local papers, *Exchange & Mart* and other specialist and non-specialist publications. They are also sold by boatyards and builders who have taken them in part exchange, and by brokers, who do not own the boats they sell but act as agents for the owner.

There is a thriving market in secondhand boats and a wide choice of craft available from all these sources. Unfortunately, no reliable guide to prices exists because differences in equipment, condition and usage can make one five-year-old boat worth twice as much as its contemporary sister ship. It will pay to look at as many boats as possible; only then will you know whether the one you decide to buy is worth the price being asked.

Start looking locally. The expense of travelling to the other end of the country to see boats that turn out to be quite unsuitable soon mounts up. Not only that, but should you buy a boat in York and want to keep it on the Thames you will have a very long delivery trip ahead of you.

When you have found what you are looking for, don't make an offer on the spot. Go back for a second look with a knowledgeable friend in tow and examine the boat from stem to stern, lifting up floorboards, delving deep into lockers and testing doors, windows, guardrails. Have a look round the engine compartment – a dirty and untidy one probably indicates a lack of attention – and give the engine a test run. Check the operation of every piece of mechanical, electrical or electronic equipment. Make a nuisance of yourself; it is a rare seller who will agree to put right faults you find after the sale has been agreed.

For all but the cheapest secondhand craft you would do well to consider employing a surveyor, and if you are borrowing money on the security of the boat this may be a condition imposed by the lender. A professional surveyor will have the knowledge to find osmosis, corrosion or rot where you might not dream of looking. He will know what faults are likely to lead to future problems and which can be safely ignored. He will also be able to give you some idea of the cost of remedial work.

Surveys do not come cheap, especially if the boat has to be lifted out for a below-the-waterline hull inspection. But they can save you money, and give you the security of knowing that if something unexpected does crop up afterwards you can get redress from the surveyor if you can prove that he has been negligent. Unless you can prove misrepresentation, or that the boat is not fit for the purpose for which it was bought, you have no such comeback on the seller, or even the broker, whose terms of business usually include a phrase saying something like: 'It is the responsibility of the purchaser to satisfy himself as to the condition of the boat'.

It makes sense to get a local surveyor to cut down on expenses and travelling time to and from the boat, for which you will be charged. The Yacht Brokers, Designers and Surveyors Association (see the Appendix at the end of this book) can supply a list of names and addresses.

If you buy a boat through a broker, the owner will be paying up to 10 per cent of its value for the broker's services. This rather high fee – after all, estate agents charge only 2 per cent or less – is justified by the brokers on the grounds that they do more work than estate agents for items of (generally) lower value. Since the asking price will probably have been adjusted upwards to take into account the broker's fee, you are effectively footing the bill. So make the broker work for his money: insist on the sale contract being drawn up in accordance with the contract offered by the British Marine Industries Federation, which sets out terms that are fair to both buyer and seller, and gives the buyer a chance to have faults remedied before the sale is completed.

Financing

It has never been easier to borrow money to buy a boat, with banks and finance houses falling over each other to lend large sums to new as well as existing customers. With such a choice it pays to shop around for the best deal.

Banks usually offer the best terms, so it is worth making your first call to your friendly local branch manager. You may be offered a personal loan at a flat, fixed rate, or a loan at a rate linked to the bank's base rate.

River cruisers on Oulton Broad.

Make sure you know whether interest is charged on the whole of the original loan or just on the reducing balance; the difference makes an 11-per-cent flat-rate loan more expensive than a 15-per-cent reducing-balance loan.

Whether you are asked for security will depend on the amount you need, the term of the loan and your personal circumstances. Unsecured loans are invariably more expensive because the bank has to carry the extra risk. A second charge on your house is the simplest form of security to arrange, but if you have blue-chip shares or gilts that you will not be selling for a few years the bank will usually accept these.

A bank will also accept a life assurance policy as security, but only for a proportion of its current surrender value. You may find that the terms of the policy allow you to get a bigger loan from the insurance company.

Finance houses can usually offer longer-term loans than banks, ten years being common on a loan secured against a second charge on your home. They charge more than banks, sometimes on a flat rate, sometimes on a reducing balance.

It may be possible to use the boat itself as security for the loan. This is called a marine mortgage, and is available from some companies specializing in boat finance whose addresses are given in the Appendix. If you do buy on a mortgage, the lender will almost certainly demand that the boat be registered under the 1894 Merchant Shipping Act so that his interest can be noted on the Deed of Registry (see below).

When you have established what the various potential lenders can offer you, draw up a table showing what your repayments are going to be over the whole term of the loan (with variable-rate loans assume that the rate will stay the same, as you will not be able to predict fluctuations with any accuracy – even the banks cannot do so). Then add on the extra costs that you would incur in each case: arrangement fees, house or registration survey fees, and so on. The totals for each loan are likely to be very different.

Registration

Any boat can be registered under the Merchant Shipping Act of 1894, but this is an involved and expensive process (costing around £250) as it requires a full survey to be carried out by a classification society surveyor. What you get for your money is a Deed of Registry that proves your title to the boat, and gives details of anyone else with a pecuniary interest in it. For inland waterways craft full registration is only likely to be necessary if you are financing the purchase by means of a marine mortgage.

Rather less expensive is the Small Ships Register run by the Royal Yachting Association. This was developed after the French made a fuss about unregistered British boats entering France. It does not prove ownership, since the details on the registration certificate consist solely of information provided by the applicant, so it is unlikely to be acceptable to lenders. Still, the French do accept it, and it costs just £10. Company-owned boats and those of over 24 metres (78 feet) in length are not eligible for Small Ships Register certification.

Insurance

Many and varied are the companies that have come unstuck on marine insurance. Underwriters have a difficult calculation to make, balancing premium income against claims, and in the past they have often got it wrong. Indeed, most companies claim that their marine insurance business actually makes a loss, despite some swingeing increases in premiums over recent years.

The boat owner thus has a difficult choice. If he goes for the lowest premium, he runs the risk that the insurers may be tiresome when he comes to make a claim. The only answer is to go for a reputable company – preferably one from which a boat-owning friend has already had experience of claiming – and to read the small print of the policy very carefully. Specialist marine insurance brokers and companies are likely to offer better terms than companies whose main business is car or household insurance; some addresses are given in the Appendix at the end of this book.

One way of reducing the premium quite considerably is to agree to an excess of, say, £50. Knowing that they will not be troubled by an endless series of small claims seems to make underwriters feel positively generous, and the excess may reduce your premiums by as much as 25 per cent.

If you borrow money to finance the purchase, you may find that the bank/finance house insists on the boat being insured comprehensively. Other than this there is no legal obligation to insure a boat at all, but you would be foolish not to take out third party insurance for a considerable sum, as the amount of damage your £10,000 narrowboat can do to a line of moored boats is limited only by your imagination. This is an extreme case, but you should view £100,000 third party insurance as a practical minimum.

As with all insurance, you should fill in the proposal form with scrupulous honesty. Any omission may invalidate the cover. Be sure to check whether such equipment as outboard motors, radios and personal effects are covered. Some might be, some not, in which case you should either ask for them to be included or arrange separate cover.

Mooring

Unless you buy a trailable cruiser which you can keep in your garden at home, you will have to find somewhere permanent to moor it. This is easier said than done. Although you can stop overnight practically anywhere but on private property, long-term mooring is strictly controlled. As waterways cruising has become more popular, the banks of rivers and canals have gradually filled up with moored craft wherever this is allowed, and these authorized permanent moorings only rarely become available to new tenants.

If you are very lucky you might find a secondhand boat for sale complete with mooring, but otherwise you will have to turn up a mooring by yourself. Start by asking the local boatyards; some have

A sense of perspective: wide and narrow canal boats.

their own moorings, or even a marina. Write to the water authority, and ask lock-keepers if they know of any that are likely to become vacant.

BOATS FOR SALE

It is easy to come unstuck generalizing about boat prices. Two new craft with identical hulls and engines may have price tags 100 per cent different because of differences in the standard of fitting out – the number of cabins and berths, the amount of equipment and the quality of construction. Secondhand values are even more of a minefield. Because boats are relatively durable, age matters far less than condition, which is difficult to tell without a personal inspection. One way of getting an idea of values is to look in the classified pages of boating magazines. At the end of the 1986 season the following craft, chosen at random from various journals, were for sale:

Narrowboats – New

40 feet, all steel, part fitted out, 1.5-litre BMC diesel	£14,995
47 feet, 2/4 berths, all steel, suitable residential use	20,000
59 feet, 6/8 berths, all steel, Lister diesel	11,000

Narrowboats – Secondhand

25 feet, 2/4 berths, all steel, with outboard engine	£4,950
26 feet, 2/4 berths, with Sabb 10hp diesel, repainted last year	5,500
36 feet, 2 berths, 1.5-litre BMC diesel, built 1981	6,950
36 feet, 4/6 berths, built 1981, 16hp diesel, just repainted	8,500
45 feet, with Lister ST2 (20hp) diesel, refitted interior	11,950
45 feet, 3 berths, Lister SR3 diesel, steel hull, GRP top	8,750
48 feet, all steel, 1.5-litre BMC diesel, suitable residential	11,950
60 feet, 4+ berths, steel hull, wooden top, built 1971	13,500
70 feet, 2 berths, Russell Newbery diesel, suitable residential	15,800
70 feet, 12 berths, ex-hire craft, built 1984	19,500

Cruisers – New

17-foot Microplus S/503, 2 berths, excl engine	£3,300
18-foot Shetland Family Four, 2/4 berths, excl engine	4,500
20-foot Hardy Family Pilot, 2/4 berths, excl engine	6,700
23-foot Ernecraft, 4/6 berths, inc 30hp diesel inboard	10,500
28-foot Walton, 4/6 berths, inc 60hp diesel inboard	25,000

Cruisers – Secondhand

20-foot Norman, 2/4 berths, built 1978, inc 15hp outboard	£2,500
23-foot Seamaster, 2/4 berths, built 1974, inc Perkins diesel	7,000
27-foot Norman 266, 4/6 berths, built 1983, inc diesel outdrive	14,000
30-foot Broom, 4/6 berths, built 1974, twin Perkins diesels	24,750
37-foot Broom Crown, built 1980, twin diesels	49,500

CONSTRUCTION STANDARDS

The Thames Water Authority lays down minimum construction standards for boats using the river, covered in a fifteen-page appendix to the Authority's *Launch Digest*. The standards are designed basically to 'minimize the risk of danger to others through fire or explosion, particularly in locks and at congested moorings', and go into great detail about the construction and siting of anything that may be a fire risk: fuel tanks, gas cylinders, exhausts, cookers, heaters and so on. The Authority also insists that all craft carry a certain number of extinguishers depending on length, a whistle or horn and, if travelling at night, a full set of navigation lights.

Craft previously used on the Thames will obviously conform with the TWA regulations – or should do, otherwise their use is illegal – but if you are bringing a boat on to the river for the first time it is worth getting a copy of the *Launch Digest* from the Authority (the address is given in the Appendix at the end of this book) to check that it meets the requirements.

There is no such obligation on canals, although the BWB has drawn up a set of 'standards for the equipping and construction of pleasure boats and houseboats using the Board's waterways'. Compliance with these standards is mandatory for houseboats and hire craft, but not yet for privately owned cruising boats, though it may be not be long before they too have to conform.

The BWB standards are even more comprehensive than the TWA's, covering safety and emergency equipment, navigation lights, anchors, fenders, toilets, engine and battery installations, fuel and gas supplies, openings in the hull and many other matters. All are sensible measures, and in most cases you will find that new boats meet the specification given. The Board also recommends that owners refitting boats for the season make any alterations and additions necessary to bring their craft up to standard. Full details are available from the BWB at the address given in the Appendix.

4

ENGINES FOR THE WATERWAYS

Any motor boat, whether narrowboat, launch or motor cruiser, will have at least one engine to provide the power and at least one propeller to convert the power into forward motion. The one is linked to the other in an intricate package, all parts of which have to do their job if the boat is to keep going. In general, they do.

Unfortunately, or fortunately, depending on your viewpoint, Britain's waterways are not over-endowed with service stations, and there is no waterborne equivalent of the AA or RAC. So if your engine does fail, you have to get out and walk, wait for a more expert mechanic to come along, or mend it yourself. At the very least, you should be able to carry out the simply daily maintenance jobs so that your chances of an engine failure are kept to a minimum.

There are five different types of engine or motor that are used on waterways craft. One of them, the steam engine, is a rare sight nowadays, although it is currently experiencing a revival among traditionalists and there are even boatyards building brand-new steamers for river and canal use.

Electric motors, too, either inboard or outboard, are very much in the minority but are becoming more popular. Modern technology has increased the output of the motors and reduced the size of the batteries required so that recharging is neither protracted nor ruinously expensive, and there are a number of places on the waterways system where you can charter electric boats and enjoy the true peace and quiet of virtually silent progress.

All other powered craft are driven by one of three varieties of internal combustion engine, a four-stroke diesel, a four-stroke petrol or a two-stroke petrol unit. All are reciprocating engines, with pistons that are propelled along a closed chamber by a controlled explosion at one end of the chamber, and a crankshaft that converts the linear movement of the piston into rotary movement, but they operate in very different ways.

Electric motors: quiet and vibration-free power. The motors themselves are also very compact, but the batteries take up a lot of space.

DIESEL ENGINE

The diesel engine is a deserved favourite on waterways craft. Slow-revving, rugged and reliable (though noisy and prone to vibration), it is also cheaper to run than a petrol engine of equivalent power. A diesel operates on what is known as the 'compression ignition' principle, which is effectively sparkless ignition, so it does not need the complex electrical system of a petrol engine.

All diesels nowadays are four-stroke engines, which means that it takes four movements of the piston – two up, two down – to complete a

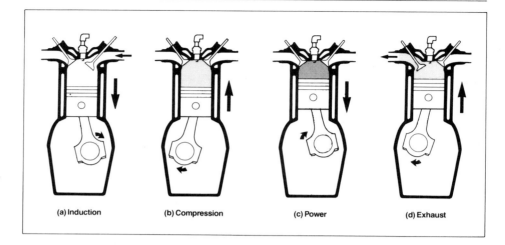

(a) Induction   (b) Compression   (c) Power   (d) Exhaust

Figure 4.1. *The four-stroke cycle, common to both petrol and diesel engines, is illustrated here in a petrol engine.*

full cycle. Figure 4.1 shows the principle of operation of a four-stroke (actually a petrol engine, the only difference being that the diesel has an injector in place of the spark plug). It may have one or a number of cylinders, each containing a piston attached to a different point on the crankshaft below. At the top of each cylinder is an inlet valve for air, an exhaust valve for burnt gases and an injector that forces in the fuel.

The first stroke of the cycle is the induction stroke, when the inlet valve opens and the piston starts travelling down the cylinder, sucking air through the valve as it does. When the piston reaches the bottom of its run the valve closes once more and the compression stroke begins. Now the piston starts travelling up the cylinder again, progressively compressing the air inside it to around a twentieth of its former volume.

This compression is twice as much as that found in petrol engines, which is one of the reasons for diesels being heavier and more expensive. It raises the temperature of the air enormously (remember Boyle's Law?), to over 1,000°F (538°C) by the time the piston has finished its upstroke. As this happens, a mixture of fuel and air is blown out in a fine spray into the combustion chamber. The instant it hits the superheated air in the cylinder it ignites, expanding and driving the piston downwards once more on its power stroke.

The power stroke is followed by the exhaust stroke, when the cylinder's exhaust valve opens and the piston travelling upwards again expels all the burnt gas and air. The piston reaches the top, the exhaust valve closes, the inlet valve opens, and the cycle begins again.

The fuel delivery system is the most critical component of a diesel. Not only does the fuel have to be injected at precisely the right moment, it also has to be delivered to the combustion chamber in the right quantity and at the right pressure – and since it is being injected into a pressurized atmosphere, that means more than 7,000psi. Pumps and injectors rarely go wrong, which is what makes the diesel so reliable, but when they do it is a specialist's job to repair them.

Because fuel supply is so critical to the smooth operation of a diesel it is vital that the oil being pumped through is free of dirt, water and air bubbles. This means filtering the supply for dirt and water and bleeding the system of any air that gets in. Under normal circumstances a filter/agglomerator will take care of the first, while the second will only be necessary if the system is dismantled or if the engine is allowed to run out of fuel. That having been said, you should take care not to allow water into the tank. Any that gets through to the injectors could very quickly lead to an expensive repair.

Like all engines a diesel runs at a high temperature, and needs efficient cooling and lubrication systems to keep the temperature down to the optimum. As there is little difference between similar systems on petrol and diesel inboards, these will be dealt with in a later, separate section.

Getting the engine to normal operating temperature as quickly as possible after start-up is important, so most modern diesels are fitted with glowplug heating that preheats the air being drawn into each cylinder. When switching on you therefore have to wait a few seconds before operating the starter.

LEFT *Many boat engines are automotive diesels, 'marinized' by specialist companies. This BL taxi engine is a popular subject for conversion. Note the two separate banks of batteries, one for engine starting and one for the services, and the gas bottle stowage near the stern.*

RIGHT *Another diesel popular on narrowboats, the Lister. Note the simple pillar-type engine control box and the diesel-powered accommodation heater on the right.*

Still found on some older narrowboats, the single-cylinder Bolinder 'hot-bulb' diesel.

The days of the crank-started engine are thankfully over, and virtually all diesels now have an electric starter motor that turns the flywheel to get the pistons moving up and down in their appointed cycles. This is the single least reliable component of the engine, whether because the motor itself packs up or because the battery on which it depends is drained. See page 67 for further information on batteries.

Some diesels are turbocharged. This is a useful way of getting more horsepower from the same engine capacity, and uses some of the exhaust pressure to drive a pump that feeds more air into the chambers so that more fuel can be burnt. Turbos are rare on waterways craft, which do not need the extra power.

Another reason for the diesel's reliability and longevity – fifty-year-old engines are still in commission in boats all over the world – is its slow revving. Most diesels used on inland waterways craft operate at 3,000rpm or less, a lot faster than those of fifty years ago but still slower than petrol engines, and many charter boat engines are governed to keep the revs below that. High-speed diesels operating at up to

4,000rpm, though increasingly common on coastal craft, are rarely seen inland except on the bigger rivers.

Apart from reliability, economy is the major feature of a diesel. Although they are much more expensive than petrol engines of equivalent power, diesel engines burn something like three quarters of the fuel – around half a gallon (2.2 litres) per 10hp per hour. Marine diesel is also cheaper than petrol by a significant margin, so the cost of each mile can be reduced by as much as half.

FOUR-STROKE PETROL ENGINE

This is the type of engine you are most likely to have in your car. As with the diesel, the four-stroke petrol engine has a piston that travels up and down each cylinder, with two upstrokes and two downstrokes per cycle. How this principle is put into operation is somewhat different.

In a petrol engine, the induction stroke starts with an inlet valve opening in the combustion chamber so that the piston on its way down draws in a mixture of fuel and air from the carburettor. The valve closes as the piston reaches the bottom of its stroke, and the piston travelling up again compresses the mix (the compression stroke). As the piston reaches the top, an electric current is delivered from the ignition system to the spark plug, and a spark arcs across the gap between the plug's electrodes. This ignites the pressurized fuel/air mixture, which drives the piston down again on its power stroke. The final, exhaust stroke of the cycle comes when the exhaust valve in the combustion chamber opens and the piston travelling up again expels the burnt gases.

Timing is again critical with a petrol engine, but so are a number of other elements in its operation. The fuel has to be delivered in the right quantity, which is the job of the carburettor; the distributor has to produce a spark at the plug electrodes at precisely the right moment; the engine has to be kept lubricated and cooled. Against this can be set the fact that many of the problems likely to crop up can be dealt with by an amateur with a modest knowledge and a small kit of tools and spares.

Petrol engines, even modern ones, are less economical than diesels, and can be reckoned to use at least 5, sometimes 6 pints (3 to 3.5 litres) per 10hp per hour. The more inflammable fuel also makes them less inherently safe.

TWO-STROKE PETROL ENGINE

A much simpler form of petrol engine, the two-stroke uses its own piston or pistons as valves. This enables it to lubricate itself, because the fuel passes through or over all the moving parts of the engine. Two-strokes therefore have oil added to the petrol, either by premixing in the fuel tank or by using a separate oil tank that measures out and dispenses the correct amount before it gets to the carburettor.

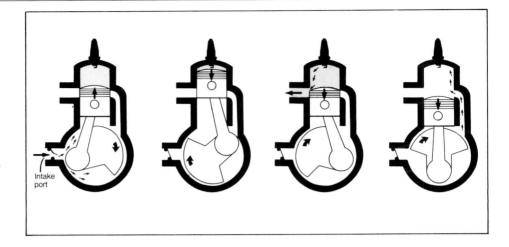

Figure 4.2. *The two-stroke cycle achieves the four basic functions of induction, compression, power and exhaust with just two movements of the piston.*

Figure 4.2 shows the principle of operation. Despite its name, a two-stroke still has to go through the same four processes that a four-stroke does – induction, compression, power and exhaust – and it does this by performing two functions at once using the piston.

Instead of valves, the two-stroke has ports to let fuel in and exhaust out. There are three of these: an inlet port in the crankcase, an exhaust port in one wall of the cylinder and a scavenger or transfer port on the opposite cylinder wall that connects the crankcase with the combustion chamber. As the piston travels up and down the cylinder it progressively masks or clears the two upper ports, while the bottom one is opened and closed automatically by a one-way reed valve.

At the beginning of the cycle, the piston is at its lowest point and there is a charge of fuel (actually a petrol/oil/air mixture) in the combustion chamber. On the upstroke, the crown of the piston passes and masks the two upper ports and then starts to compress the fuel. At the same time, by expanding the effective volume of the lower chamber, it creates a low-pressure zone in the crankcase. This opens the reed valve and draws another charge of fuel in the lower chamber. Thus induction and compression are covered in the same stroke.

As the piston reaches the top of its stroke, a spark ignites the mix and the piston is propelled downwards. The crown clears the exhaust port first, allowing the burnt gases to escape, and then the scavenging port. The underside of the piston is meanwhile pressurizing the fuel mix in the crankcase, closing the reed valve, so that when the scavenger port is cleared the full charge is expelled into the upper chamber.

Because a two-stroke engine has no valve gear it can be made much lighter and more cheaply than a four-stroke. For cheap, lightweight power it has no peer, but it does suffer from two real drawbacks: it is noisy, and expensive to run – not only is the fuel dearer because of the added oil, but consumption is considerably higher, at about 1 gallon (4.5 litres) per 10hp per hour.

TRANSMISSION

Whatever engine is used, it has to be connected to a propeller via some form of drive before its power can be converted into propulsion. There are four basic methods of achieving this: shaft drive, outdrive, outboard and water jet. Shaft-drive installations are often referred to simply as inboards, which can be a little confusing, as both outdrives and water jets are coupled to inboard engines.

Shaft Drive

Simplest of all, and most common on waterways craft, is the shaft drive. This consists of a gearbox coupled to the engine, which may be any of the three basic types covered above, and a shaft leading from gearbox to prop. The gearbox will usually be of the reverse reduction type: that is to say, it brings the revs of the engine down to the required level so that, for example, every two turns of the crankshaft produce one turn of the propeller; and it offers a means of reversing the direction of rotation of the shaft to provide astern propulsion.

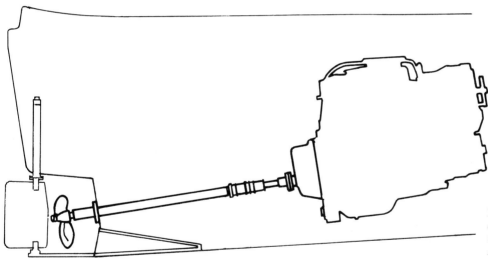

Figure 4.3. *The conventional (shaft drive) inboard installation on a single-engined motor cruiser.*

Marine gearboxes are simpler than their equivalents in cars, operating at a single drive ratio in either forward or reverse and with no separate clutch control, although most have a switch that disengages the drive. The helmsman changes gear either with a combined throttle/gearshift or a separate three-position gearshift lever.

There are again several different forms of shaft drive. In-line transmission, as its name suggests, keeps the crankshaft of the engine, the shaft and the propeller all in one line. Since most hull designs call for the shaft to leave the hull at a slight angle from the horizontal, this means that the engine itself has to be installed at an angle.

An alternative if the engine has to be installed horizontally – say, to keep the height of the engine compartment down – is to use a down angle gearbox, whose output shaft is set at an angle to the input shaft, or to incorporate some form of flexible drive coupling in the drive train.

Less common on waterways craft is the V-drive. This has a second gearbox in the middle of the shaft between the engine and the prop; the shaft enters and leaves the gearbox on the same side, forming the 'V' of the name and allowing the engine to be mounted further aft than it would be with an in-line installation. The engine also has to be installed back to front, with the gearbox at the forward end and the primary shaft leading forwards.

Another variation of the shaft drive is the hydraulic drive. In this the engine is used to run a hydraulic pump feeding a hydraulic motor on the end of the prop shaft. The advantage of this system is that power is routed through flexible pipes, allowing the engine to be installed anywhere on the boat.

Two ends of a hydraulic drive system. This avoids many of the problems of aligning and installing a conventional shaft-drive inboard, and allows the engine to be fitted anywhere on board, at any angle.

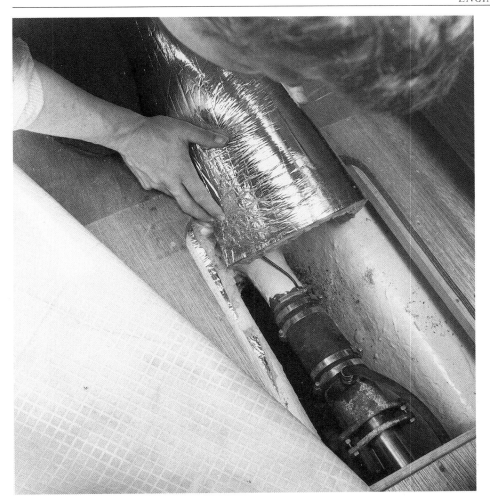

Stern gland assembly on an inboard-engined river cruiser. The foam reduces shaft noise in the aft cabin.

However the transmission is arranged, a shaft has to pass through the hull at some point. This point is invariably below the waterline, which presents a problem: how do you keep a watertight seal between spinning shaft and static hull? The answer is the stern gland, a collar of grease and packing compound around the shaft at the inboard end of the stern tube.

Inboard boats are steered using a rudder that depends on water flowing over its surface to be effective. Under forward power this is no problem, because the propeller is immediately ahead of the rudder driving a stream of water past it. Going astern, the effect is less pronounced – the prop is sucking the water past the rudder rather than driving it – while with the prop in neutral you are dependent entirely on the momentum of the boat to keep steerage way. Nevertheless, since steerage is a function of boat speed and rudder area, a large rudder can ensure you retain steerage way until the boat is almost stopped.

Because they project from the hull, the shaft and propeller of an inboard-engined boat need protection from grounding. In a single installation the keel will usually provide this protection, but twin-engined boats with their offset sterngear are rather more vulnerable – a point to bear in mind when you are considering a three-point turn that involves reversing up towards a river or canal bank.

Protected from grounding or not, the propellers of boats that use Britain's rivers and canals only too regularly pick up tangles of weed, rope or polythene that bring progress to an abrupt halt. When this happens, especially on a fast-flowing river, it is important to clear the obstruction as soon as possible. Many inboard-engined waterways craft therefore have a weed hatch directly above the propeller, a piece of trunking leading from above the waterline to a cut-out in the hull bottom. Opening the hatch will give access to the prop.

Outdrive

Another way of transmitting the power of an inboard engine to the propeller is an outdrive, a form of articulated leg that provides not only propulsion but also steering. Outdrive boats have their engines installed well aft, coupled directly to the outdrive, which is bolted on to the transom. Either diesel or four-stroke petrol engines may be used.

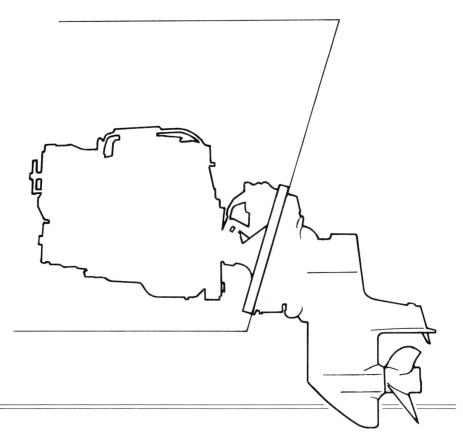

Figure 4.4. *A typical outdrive installation.*

The outdrive – also known variously as the sterndrive, inboard-outboard or Z-drive – is at the same time a gearbox, a shaft and a rudder. Drive is transmitted from the engine via a shaft to a reverse reduction gearbox outside the boat, then through two sets of bevel gears and two more shafts to the propeller. As with shaft-drive inboard installations, throttle and gear control are by means of a combination lever near the helm.

With a shaft-drive inboard the position of the propeller is fixed, but on an outdrive the whole external unit can be turned through 30–40 degrees, thus altering the direction of thrust of the prop. Some models also have power trim-tilt, which makes clearing a fouled propeller relatively simple.

This arrangement makes for extremely responsive steering in either ahead or astern gear, but has one major drawback, which is that the effect relies entirely on prop thrust: the surface area of the bottom unit is very small in comparison with that of a rudder and so you lose virtually all steerage the moment the prop stops turning.

Because an outdrive leaves the transom at water level you need some form of seal, though nothing as complicated as a stern gland. This is usually a rubber membrane called the bellows, fixed firmly to both transom and leg, that keeps out the water but allows the leg full movement from side to side or – if power tilt is fitted – up and down.

Outdrives are most likely to be met on river and Broads-type cruisers. They are not suitable for narrowboats or other boats without transoms, and in general are too powerful for waterways craft of under about 20 feet in length, where an outboard is a better proposition.

A low-powered variation on this theme is the saildrive, originally invented for sailing boats. Here the engine is mounted in the after part of the boat, driving a propeller via a leg that projects through the bottom of the hull. It is not generally found on waterways craft, its position making the propeller very vulnerable and difficult to clear should it pick up weed.

Outboard

For smaller boats especially, an outboard provides an ideal source of power. Although production models of up to more than 200hp are available, the majority of outboard-driven river and canal boats will need engines of less than 15 or 20hp.

An outboard is a self-contained engine/transmission package – bolt-on power, to use one description. Mounted in a special well, or more usually on the transom or a transom bracket, it consists of an engine turned on its side and driving a propeller via a vertical shaft. At the end of the shaft is a lower unit with bevel gears that rotate the drive through 90 degrees.

Like the outdrive, the outboard provides steering as well as propulsion, with a propeller that can be turned to give directional thrust. The helmsman steers using either a tiller on the front of the

Packaged power for a 26-foot river cruiser: a 30hp outboard.

engine (especially on smaller boats with smaller engines) or a conventional wheel connected to the motor by hydraulic or wire cables. Throttle settings are controlled either by a twist-grip on the tiller or a remote unit mounted by the helm. As with the outdrive, steerage is entirely dependent on a few revs at the prop.

The majority of outboards have a forward-neutral-reverse gearbox, but some smaller models have 360-degree steering, which makes a gearbox unnecessary as the whole engine can be turned through 180 degrees to give reverse thrust.

Weed is not generally a problem with outboards, as the engine can simply be tilted out of the water to clear the prop. However, to protect the blades from damage most smaller models have a shear pin that breaks if the spinning prop hits an obstruction. This can happen with monotonous regularity on some shallower waterways with tree branches and old prams lurking just below the surface, and it pays to carry several spares.

The most common powerhead among outboards is a two-stroke, which makes them relatively cheap, light and simple to service or repair, but often noisy and always expensive to run. Four-stroke models are available in the Honda and Yamaha ranges, a number of US manufacturers make electric outboards, and the Italian company Ruggerini has a diesel model.

Water Jet

Less popular in Britain than on the Continent, the water jet deserves a mention as it is ideal for shallow, weed-infested waters. A standard inboard engine is connected via a gearbox to an impeller mounted in a tube at the aft end of the hull bottom. The impeller draws in water from the front of the tube and drives it aft through a jet nozzle, producing a much more concentrated thrust than can be obtained with a propeller. A forward-neutral-reverse gearbox and rudder are unnecessary, as the direction of thrust can be adjusted and even reversed using a sort of bucket that diverts the jetstream as it leaves the nozzle.

The impeller on a water-jet is likely to be lighter and more fragile than the propeller of other drive units, but as it does not protrude from the hull it is well protected. A strainer at the forward end of, the water intake will usually prevent weed or other rubbish from being sucked into the tube.

ENGINE SYSTEMS

In addition to their transmissions, all engines have several other systems that are essential if they are to function correctly. These include cooling, fuel delivery, exhaust, starting, lubrication and, in the case of petrol engines, ignition.

Cooling

Any type of internal combustion engine will operate most efficiently at a given temperature that varies from engine to engine. This temperature is reached within a matter of minutes after start-up, but the process of combustion and the internal friction caused by components moving against each other continually add more heat and it is important for this extra heat to be removed as it is generated.

Happily, boats are surrounded by an inexhaustible supply of a supremely effective cooling medium, water. If channels are cast into the engine block and cold water pumped through them, the water as it leaves the block will take away the heat. This 'water jacket' principle is common to all three of the usual forms of water cooling found on boats: direct, indirect and keel cooling.

Simplest of the three is direct or raw water cooling. This, as its name implies, is where the water for the water jacket is drawn directly from outside the boat, pumped round the engine block and then back overboard. It is not generally used on boats that operate near or on the coast or offshore, as the corrosive effect of the hot salt water would spell a very short life for the engine. On waterways craft, however, this is not a problem. Nevertheless, it is the least common of the three because of another drawback: as there is no reservoir of cooling water, a temporary interruption in the water supply, caused for example by a weed-blocked intake, would lead to instant overheating.

More popular in marine engines, especially on seagoing boats, is indirect cooling. With this system the engine is cooled by a permanent freshwater jacket that is in turn cooled by raw water supplied from outside the boat. The raw water – salt or fresh – passes through a heat exchanger, as does the fresh water from the engine block. Heat is transferred from the one to the other, the fresh water is circulated back to the block and the raw water is pumped back overboard. There is a certain amount of loss of cooling water through evaporation, but a header tank provides a reservoir in case of need.

Indirect cooling is still dependent on an adequate supply of water from outside, and again is susceptible to blockage. The third alternative is subject to no such restrictions, which is why it is popular among inland waterways craft. Keel cooling requires no water from outside the boat; the water circulating round the block is pumped through a tube or series of tubes along the base of the hull, and the heat dissipates into the plating and the water outside.

Both indirect and keel cooling require a header tank that has to be kept topped up with fresh water, and all three forms need a pump to circulate the water round the engine. The pump will be driven by a belt led down to a pulley on the end of the crankshaft, and as long as this is kept at the correct tension there should be no problems unless the pump itself breaks down. It is important to check that the water is indeed circulating: this can be done with direct and indirect systems by looking over the side to see that there is a steady stream of water coming out of the cooling outlet (with a wet exhaust, the outlet will be the exhaust pipe – see page 66). With keel cooling systems the best idea is to keep an eye on the temperature gauge.

Some waterways boats are powered by air-cooled engines. Air cooling is much simpler than any of the water-cooled arrangements, with a fan that directs a blast of air over cooling fins projecting from the block. The fins take heat from the block, and the air whisks the heat away. As long as there is an unobstructed supply of air to the fan, and the fan keeps working, the system is foolproof (if noisy).

Fuel Supply

As mentioned earlier, the supply of exactly metered quantities of clean fuel, critical to the functioning of a diesel engine, is achieved through a system of injectors, pumps and filters. There are at least two filters – one a sedimenter to remove larger bits of dirt and droplets of water, the other an agglomerator that removes even tiny droplets. Because air has to be kept out of the system, any maintenance work that involves dismantling a component will mean bleeding the system afterwards.

A unique feature of the diesel engine is that more fuel than necessary is pumped through to the injectors. This helps lubricate the injector pump and the injectors themselves. What is not needed for combustion is then returned to the tank.

Four-stroke petrol engines are not as choosy about their fuel supply, but this is still filtered on its way from tank to carburettor. The fuel delivery system is altogether simpler, and minor adjustments can be made to the carburettor, which mixes petrol and air and feeds the mixture to the engine in quantities determined by the throttle setting. Filters should always be changed at the intervals stated in the owner's handbook, and sedimenters drained of the water and dirt they have collected.

The oil that has to be blended with petrol in two-stroke engines can be introduced in one of two ways – either premixed in the tank, or by means of a separate oil tank that dispenses the correct amount into the fuel line as required. It is important with premixed fuel to get the right proportions: too little oil, and the moving parts will not be lubricated properly; too much, and the unburnt oil will be ejected in a cloud of black smoke from the exhaust. Two-strokes have a similar carburettor to that used on four-stroke engines and again this can be adjusted to improve running.

Inboard engines are fed from separate tanks built into the boat, and in the case of twin installations the tank for each engine is often cross-connected to the other so that any permutation of tank and engine is possible. If this is not done and, say, the port engine fails, you will only be able to draw from the starboard tank, which both reduces range and affects trim.

Engine control panel and other switchgear on a narrowboat.

Fuel gauges for built-in tanks are sometimes fitted on the instrument panel; narrowboats rarely have such refinements, however, and the amount of fuel remaining in the tank is generally measured using a dipstick inserted through the filler pipe or another aperture in the top.

Smaller outboards have their own integral fuel tanks, but larger models are fed from in-built or portable tanks, in most cases with sight gauges to indicate the amount of fuel remaining.

Exhaust

All internal combustion engines produce hot, acid gases which have to be removed from the boat as quickly and safely as possible. In outboards, which have a toe in the water, so to speak, this is simple: the gases are led down the outboard leg and out underwater, in some cases through the propeller boss to give extra forward thrust.

The problem is more complex with inboard installations. Because the engine is well inside the boat, a length of piping is needed to carry the gases away, and this has to be either cooled or heavily insulated to prevent it setting fire to the rest of the boat. For this reason most pleasure boat installations use a 'wet exhaust' system, where the raw cooling water, after passing through the engine heat exchanger, is injected into the exhaust. Even though it is by now quite hot, the water can carry away much of the heat from the exhaust before it exits through the exhaust outlet, and it also helps to reduce the noise from a dry bark to a burble.

All exhaust pipes, wet and dry, are hot, so nothing should ever be stowed in a position where it can fall against them.

Starter

Except for a few diesels and smaller outboards, modern engines are started electrically with a starter motor that sets the flywheel turning. This puts you in rather a spot if the starter motor fails to work, but unfortunately the manual alternative start has now virtually disappeared, as it has on cars. Starting both electric and manual engines is covered in Chapter 5.

Lubrication

Friction would soon cause the moving parts of an engine to overheat and seize if they were not separated from each other by a film of oil. In a four-stroke engine this oil bath is constantly being pumped up from the sump to the bearings, then through the block to the cylinder head; it then runs over the valve gear, draining down through the block and back into the sump again. Always watch the oil pressure gauge; low pressure may mean that you need to add more or change the filter. If that does not do the trick, the oil pump may be faulty.

Two-strokes need no separate lubrication, but like the four-stroke their gearcases have to be kept topped up, again to prevent friction welding the gears together.

Ignition

The spark that ignites the fuel/air mixture in petrol engines comes from a high-voltage electric current arcing across the gap between two electrodes of a spark plug. This current is generated by a coil, passed to a distributor and then sent to each of the plugs in turn. This complexity, and the well-known aphorism that water and electricity do not mix, put a lot of boat owners off petrol engines, but generally speaking they are reliable provided the ignition system itself is kept dry. Water-repellent sprays such as WD40 can often dry off wet electrodes or points and get a reluctant engine going.

The Electrical System

Any boat that depends on a battery to start the engine and also needs power for lighting or other domestic services should have two batteries or banks of batteries, connected so that the engine-start battery can never be flattened by overuse of the services. Twin-engined boats should have one bank for the services and starting one engine, and one exclusively for starting the other.

The batteries depend for their charge on an alternator or dynamo driven by a belt which must be kept at the right tension, allowing half an inch of play in the belt to keep it tight round the generator without damaging the bearings.

Car batteries are not suitable for marine use, because the special circumstances of a boat – the damp, the long periods of non-use and the not infrequent flattening of the battery – demand a high-capacity, heavy-duty unit. Lead acid batteries are usually fitted, but the more expensive manganese alkaline type may also be used.

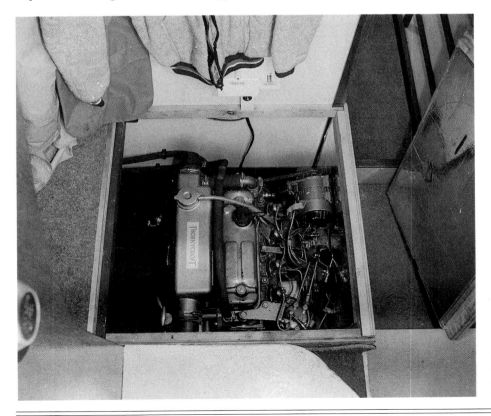

Easy access to the engine compartment for daily checks and maintenance work is essential.

5

STARTING OUT

It is very tempting when writing about boats to draw analogies with cars, as cars are altogether more familiar to the average reader. There are, it is true, certain similarities between the two, but almost none when it comes to operation and handling.

One important difference crops up the instant you step aboard a boat, keys in hand. Your car handbook probably gives a list of checks you should carry out each day, each week and each month. Unless you are unusually conscientious, you will forgo at least the daily checks. You simply assume that everything works as intended. If something goes wrong you can always pull into the side of the road and call out the garage, the AA or the RAC.

Boats are another matter, however. It was mentioned in an earlier chapter that there is no waterways AA to get you out of trouble should your boat engine break down. This fact, and the fact that most boats lie unused for weeks or months at a time, make it imperative that you carry out a series of basic checks every time you take the boat out – no matter how casually you treat your car.

So, every time you take a boat out of mothballs, you should ask yourself two questions: is it safe, and will it get me where I want to go? The prestart checks are designed to answer those questions.

SAFETY

The first and most important consideration is fire. With sometimes large stocks of volatile fuel and bottles of inflammable gas aboard, a boat inevitably presents a fire risk. Gas leaks can usually be detected by smell, fuel leaks with a quick inspection of the bilges. Do not switch on the power supply, light a cigarette or start the engine until you have verified that there has not been a leak in your absence.

Second on the list is whether the boat is watertight. Wooden and, to a lesser extent, steel boats can let in water through their seams, but even glassfibre hulls have skin fittings such as cooling water intakes that may become detached or damaged. Again this can usually be shown up with a bilge inspection.

Skin fittings are fixed and immobile, so they can be tightened well down and sealed with mastic, but every inboard-engined boat will have one hole in the hull bottom that cannot be permanently sealed in the same way. This is the hole, invariably below the waterline, through which the propeller shaft leaves the hull.

The aft end of the shaft is housed in a stern tube, which does not move in relation to the hull and can therefore be firmly fixed in place to prevent water getting in between tube and hull. The shaft, on the other hand, has to be free to rotate within the tube but not loose enough to let in water. As mentioned earlier, this apparent paradox is resolved with a stern gland at the forward end of the stern tube, a ring of packing and compacted grease that seals the gap between tube and shaft yet at the same time allows the shaft to rotate.

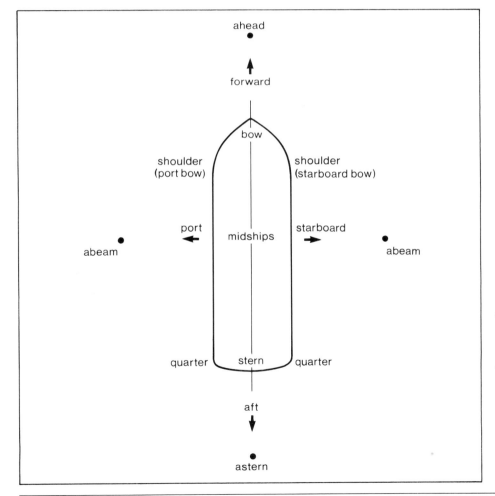

Figure 5.1. *A basic glossary. The mariner's vocabulary may seem obscure, but like any jargon it has its uses as a form of verbal shorthand that explains exactly what is meant without the need for further clarification. The term 'port', for example, does not just mean 'left' but 'on your left when facing in the direction in which the boat is heading'. If you turn round and face the stern, the port quarter is the one on your right.*

The diagram shows a few of the more common terms used to indicate direction.

Over a period of time the grease packing in the stern gland gradually escapes, so more has to be fed in to keep up the pressure. This is usually done with a screw-down stern gland greaser, which should be given a single complete turn every day the boat is in use.

Outdrives leave the hull through the transom rather than underneath the boat, but they can still let water in if the bellows that forms a seal between the drive and the transom perishes or tears. Check that the seal is still good.

Having established that your boat is neither going to catch fire or sink, the next question is whether it will get you where you want to go. Turn on the battery master switch – usually in the battery compartment – and then the individual switches on the console by the helm. Check the operation of all the electrics: lights (inside and outside), wipers, horn, bilge pump, water pump and so on.

Now the fuel: if there is an electric fuel gauge, turn on the instruments – they may be separately switched, or you may have to turn the ignition key a single click to the right – and check the level. If you do not have a gauge by the helm, there may be a visible sight gauge on the tank, or you may have to dip the tank with a dipstick (often no more than a piece of wood).

Any indirect water-cooled inboard engine, petrol or diesel, will have a header tank that supplies the water for the cooling jacket. Remove the radiator-type cap on the top of this tank, check the level and top up to the mark if necessary. Do not overfill – the water should be an inch or more below the top to allow for expansion. While in the engine compartment, check the level of electrolyte in the batteries, and top up with distilled water if necessary (some batteries are now 'sealed for life' and cannot be topped up; nor should they need to be).

With four-stroke engines, check the lubricating oil in the sump, again topping up if necessary. Some two-strokes have oil injection rather than premixed petrol/oil; with these, check the level of oil in the tank.

All engines, inboard and outboard, drive through a gearbox which should also be kept topped up with oil. Again, check the level and top up with the correct grade if necessary. Note that gear oil and engine oil may well be of different grades; use the grade specified in your handbook, and never use anything but two-stroke outboard oil for two-stroke outboard engines.

Your propeller may have attracted some weed, rope or a piece of polythene bag while the boat has been at its mooring. Open up the weed hatch for a look (see Chapter 6), or in the case of an outdrive operate the tilt mechanism to bring the lower unit out of the water. This should not be necessary with outboards, which are usually either removed from the transom for security or, if they are left in place during the owner's absence, raised clear of the water.

Having checked the main engine services, try the engine itself (see 'Starting Up' on page 73). It should not be necessary to run up the revs in neutral: besides being bad practice, many engines have a governor to

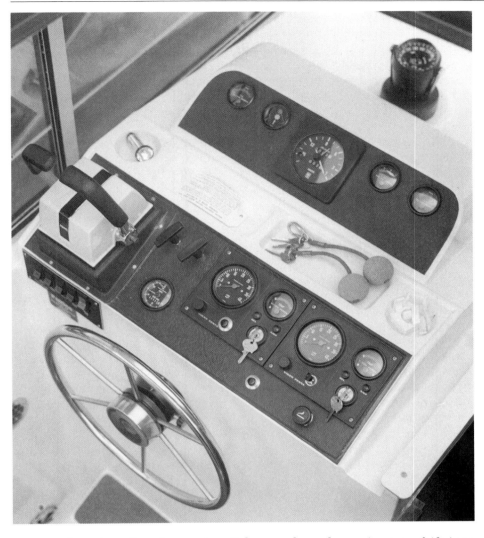

Dashboard of a twin-engined cruiser. The twin tachometers are essential for matching engine revs to avoid the need to apply permanent helm.

prevent just that. Let the engine tick over for a few minutes, shift into forward and then into astern to ensure you have drive. Provided the revs are kept low, the time in gear is kept short and the boat is well secured to the pontoon or bank, you won't be going anywhere. Shift back into neutral and, if you are not leaving immediately, turn the engine off.

Now check the steering. The worst time to find out that you have no control over the boat's direction is just after you have cast off and are heading towards another moored boat. Traditional narrowboats and some other waterways craft will have simple tiller steering. As the tiller is connected directly to the rudder shaft there is little that can go wrong with this set-up, but it is worth waggling the tiller and taking a look over the stern as you do to make sure that the rudder is turning.

Outboard engines, as discussed in Chapter 4, not only propel the boat along but also provide a means of steering. Lower-powered engines, up to about 15hp, can be steered by means of a tiller and although it is practically impossible for the lower unit to move independently of the powerhead, it is again worth waggling the tiller to make sure you have free movement.

Larger outboards and outdrive units require some form of geared steering, as they are too powerful for direct tiller control. This takes the form of wheel steering, linked by hydraulics or cable with a ram that turns the engine or outdrive in the required direction. Wheel steering will also be needed on inboard-engined craft where the helm is not on the aft deck, and on craft with dual helm positions.

The relative complexity of cable and hydraulic systems – relative to the direct-acting tiller, that is – makes them a potential source of problems. At the very least, each time you go aboard give the wheel a full lock-to-lock turn and either look yourself or have someone else check that the action is being mirrored at the stern. You should also check mechanical linkages regularly, to ensure that they are free to move and that the pins holding the linkages together have not dropped out. In the case of hydraulic systems, keep the master cylinder topped up with fluid.

Next, take a turn round the deck. Cleats and fairleads should be firmly fixed to the deck: you may need them not only to hold the boat at a mooring but also to stop the boat when coming alongside. Are the stanchions secure, and the guardrails tight? Loose guardrails or stanchions are worse than none at all; they can imbue a dangerous false sense of confidence in the crew.

Finally, check the inventory of safety equipment. This is something that should be done every trip as it is all too easy to forget that you took some vital piece of gear home last time. A comprehensive list is given in Chapter 8.

BUNKERING

Taking on fuel and water, or bunkering, is something that you will probably have to do each time you go out. Certainly, if the boat has been left for any time, it will be better to replace the water in the tank rather than risk giving yourself and your crew tummy aches. (Besides, stale water tastes unpleasant.) There are water points at all boatyards and marinas, and many provided by waterways authorities. Not all will have hoses, so you should carry your own on board. When refilling, it is a good idea to run the hose into the river or canal for a few seconds to get rid of the standing water before putting it into the filler pipe.

Fuel may be more difficult to get hold of when you want it – it is only when you do not need any that you pass three fuel jetties in a row – so carry a can just in case you have to walk to a garage.

The price of fuel varies significantly from one supplier to another.

This is particularly so with diesel, where the lack of tax on marine fuel makes even the highest waterside price seem a bargain compared with road diesel. If you can, it pays to shop around.

When refuelling, think 'safety'. Switch off the engine, turn off the cooker and heaters, and do not let anyone smoke on board. Built-in fuel and water tanks often have identical fillers set into the deck, the only difference between them being colour-coding – red for the former, blue for the latter – or the legends 'FUEL' or 'WATER' engraved in the metal. Be very careful, when topping up, not to contaminate one with the other, either by mistakenly opening the wrong filler or by spilling. It should be a golden rule that when one filler cap is off the other should be on. Do not assume that if you have found the fuel filler on an unfamiliar boat, the unmarked one must be water – if you have two fuel tanks, there may be two fuel fillers.

Portable fuel tanks for outboards should if possible be lifted out of the boat to be refilled (removing the empty tank is not the problem; hoisting the 50lb refilled one back in is). Though a bit of a sweat, this prevents any possibility of spillage, which is all to the good.

Integral fuel tanks are fitted to some outboards. These may take only a few pints, so be careful not to overfill – although the spillage will not go over the boat, a pint of petrol in their river will do the fish no good at all.

STARTING UP

With all checks completed, you can start off. The procedure for this depends on the engine, and the various types are covered separately below, starting with the most common.

Diesels

The engine will need electricity – unless it is a manual-start model, which is dealt with below – and a supply of fuel, so the first thing to do is to ensure that the battery master switches and the fuel tap are turned on. Check that the gear lever is in neutral and the throttle pushed forward about a quarter of the way to its stop. Many modern engines have a single-lever combined gearshift and throttle, with a disengage button either on the handle or on the central boss of the control unit. With these, depress the button while pushing the lever forward till you feel the first bit of resistance.

There may be a lever in the shape of a T-bar on the instrument panel, used to kill the engine when stopping it. If the T-bar has been pulled out, push it fully home. Now insert the key into the ignition and turn it one click to the right.

There is no choke on diesels, but most engines have a glowplug arrangement that preheats the air coming into the cylinders and prevents the first few revolutions producing nothing but a cloud of black smoke. This preheating takes place automatically and is usually indicated by an orange light on the dashboard with a stylized filament drawn on it. When the light goes off – in a matter of seconds – the engine can be started.

Now turn the key a further click to the right, or press the start button if one is fitted. The starter should turn and the engine catch. Bring the key back a click, wait a second or two to make sure that the engine has settled and throttle back. With a single-lever control, the disengage button will automatically pop out; although the engine will now be idling in forward gear, a clutch in the gearbox will prevent the prop turning until you push the throttle forward again. With a dual-lever control, throttle and gears are controlled separately, so the gear lever remains in neutral throughout the start-up operation.

Simple single-lever engine control on a narrowboat.

Besides fuel and electricity the diesel also needs lubricating oil and cooling water. Oil pressure will be shown on a gauge on the dashboard, and should be carefully monitored to ensure that it does not drop below the level shown in the handbook. On most modern engines there will be an alarm that buzzes if oil pressure falls. On hearing the buzzer you should shut down immediately and investigate the cause of the problem.

Raw water cooling systems are easy to check; if they are working properly there will be a steady stream of water from the outlet or, in the case of a wet exhaust (see Chapter 4), from the exhaust. The same applies to indirect heat exchanger cooling systems. Keel cooling is more difficult to monitor, but there will be a gauge on the dash and perhaps an alarm to warn of any sudden rise in temperature. With air-cooled engines, check that the fan is operating.

A diesel needs electricity only to start it, not to keep on running. To stop it, therefore, you not only have to bring the key back to the 'off' position but you also have to cut the fuel supply, either by pulling out the T-bar mentioned earlier or operating a separate stop button. The oil pressure warning will sound as the pressure drops, but will cut off automatically when the switch is returned to the 'off' position. Do not forget to turn off the fuel if you are not going to use the engine again for a while.

Manual-start diesels are still manufactured and are actually preferred by some users since they are quite independent of any electrical supply. With these, after turning on the fuel and opening the throttle about half-way to the stop, raise the decompression lever on top of the engine and swing the handle until the flywheel is turning at a respectable speed. Push the decompression lever down again, and the engine should rumble into life. If it does not, try again, and this time do not push the lever down until the flywheel is turning even faster. Stopping the engine is usually a simple matter of operating a separate kill button or lever.

Petrol Inboards and Outdrives

Once again, check that battery master switches and fuel taps are turned on. Disengage the gear (with a single-lever control) or put the gearshift into neutral, and ease the throttle forward to the first bite of the friction stop. Insert the ignition key, choke if necessary and turn the key two stops to the right. When the engine fires, return the key to the first position. With the engine running, check oil pressure and flow of cooling water. Stopping the engine is simply a matter of returning the key to the upright position. Again, remember to turn off the fuel.

Outboards

The procedure for electric-start outboards with remote control is similar to that for petrol inboards, except that the tank will have a vent screw that must be undone first, and it may be necessary to prime the fuel system by squeezing a bulb in the fuel line several times until the bulb is filled and becomes hard. With tiller-control engines the only difference will be that the throttle is in the form of a twist grip, and the gearshift and choke are mounted on the front plate or side of the engine.

Smaller outboards may not have electric start. Instead, a recoil starter will be fitted, mounted on top of the engine and with a rope pull attached. Again, prime the fuel system (unless the engine has an integral fuel tank, in which case gravity will do the job for you after you open the vent and the fuel tap), pull the choke and open the throttle about a quarter to a third of its travel. Then, with one hand on the top of the engine casing to prevent the whole motor from tipping up, pull the starter cord smoothly out as far as it will go. There should be no need to jerk. If the engine fails to catch, release the pull, which will automatically return to its housing, and try again. When the engine is running, check for cooling water; although the outlet will usually be underwater, there will be a thin but steady stream of water from a tell-tale vent in the shaft.

The older Seagull engine is an exception to the norm. This has a rope pull starter, but the cord has to be wound round a drum on the top of the engine. When pulled out to its full extent the cord slips off the drum, and if the engine does not fire it has to be rewound for the next start. One point to watch with these engines is that there is no one immediately behind you when you operate the starter; the end of the cord could take an eye out.

Changing Gear

Unlike in a car, you can change gear from forward to reverse in a boat without waiting for it to come to a halt. This is just as well, since under most circumstances your engine will provide the only means of braking. You should still treat the gearbox with respect — never slam a single-lever control from full ahead to full astern (or vice versa), and with dual-lever controls always haul back on the throttle before changing gear. Where possible, all throttle and gear movements should be made gently.

AND IF IT DOESN'T?

A well-maintained marine engine should not let you down, but it may not know that. The procedure for dealing with an engine that will not start is the same as that for handling any mechanical breakdown: eliminate the possible causes one by one, starting with the most obvious. What you can do yourself will depend on your knowledge and on the contents of your tool kit, but it will avoid needless expense, waste of time and embarrassment if you carry out a few basic checks.

If the engine will not respond at all to your turning the ignition key,

the problem lies in the electrics. Check that the battery master switch is on, and that there is no other switch or blown fuse that could be interrupting the circuit. Check that the gear lever is in neutral – there may be a safety interlock that prevents you starting in gear. Check that the battery terminals are secure, and inspect the cables for any sign of a break. If there is a detectable click or a whirr from the engine when you turn the key, the starter motor may be at fault – a job for the engineer.

If the engine turns, but only slowly, suspect a flat battery. This is more likely to happen if you have only one battery or bank of batteries to handle starting and services, and probably means that you have overused the services (lights and so on) while the engine was not running. Turn off every electrical appliance on board, including the lights, and try again. If the engine still refuses to turn over fast enough, you have a choice of borrowing a battery, using long jump leads to take a few amps from a neighbouring boat, or calling in an engineer.

An engine that turns over but does not fire may have a problem with fuel delivery. Check that there is fuel in the tank, that the fuel taps are on and, in the case of a portable tank, that the vent is unscrewed and the fuel line is primed. There may be a glass filter bowl, or on petrol

Interior steering position on a single-engined river cruiser. Note the disengage button at the base of the combination throttle/gearshift on the right of the dashboard.

engines a carburettor float chamber with a top that can be removed. Check that these have fuel in; if not, the pump may be failing to draw it through from the tank. The fuel filter may be blocked, in which case clearing it is a job that is within the scope of anyone who can use a screwdriver or spanner.

Diesel engines will not work if there is any air in the fuel system, and bleeding the system is covered in most owner's handbooks. Apart from that, there are few diesel fuel system repairs that can be tackled by an amateur, so if this is not the problem call in the engineer.

Petrol engines have another system to go wrong – the ignition. Here again there is a limit to what you can do without more knowledge than there is space to include here, but you can remove the spark plugs, clean them if their electrodes are fouled or replace them if they are pitted. Check the gap with a feeler gauge. The contact breaker in the distributor can also easily be checked and cleaned or replaced. Some modern engines have capacitor discharge or electronic ignition, which can only be repaired by an expert.

Cooling systems are the cause of most problems with boat engines. If there is a sudden temperature rise, check the header tank. If it needs constant topping up, this may indicate a blocked strainer in the cooling water inlet, which can be easily cleared, or a leaking hose which you may be able to tape up.

In Chapter 4 it was explained that small outboard engines, to protect their vulnerable propellers, have a shear pin that locks the prop around the shaft. If a blade hits something in the water, the pin will immediately break and the prop will lose its drive, preventing further damage. The engine handbook will explain how to replace the pin: make sure that you carry at least two spares, preferably three.

6

UNDER WAY

You have now checked the boat and started the engine. Everyone is on board. It's time to leave the berth.

On our relatively protected inland waterways the boater has an altogether easier time than he would have on coastal waters. There is no tide in most places, no swell, and for most part no waves – although on lakes such as Loch Ness the wrong wind can soon whip up a respectable sea.

But life is never simple, and even inland every boat is subject to forces of nature that will have a great bearing on how it handles. The most significant of these is wind, to which can be added current on rivers and some canals.

Boats for use on inland waterways tend towards shallow draught, and long superstructures as high as bridges allow. With limited depth over much of the system, the boat designer cannot afford to allow too great a depth of keel, and since he wants if possible to get standing headroom throughout the accommodation this will be mirrored in considerable air draught – typically, a narrowboat of 2-foot draught would have 6 feet of hull and superstructure above the waterline.

In a beam wind, this 6-foot wall is subject to tremendous sideways pressure, and although the 2-foot underwater section will present some resistance it needs a helping hand from the engine. This pressure lessens as the wind moves forward or aft, but is always there and always needs to be taken into account.

At the same time, other forces may be affecting the underwater section of the hull. These might be acting in opposition to the wind, in concert with it, or somewhere between the two. The current of a river is the most obvious, but every weir stream and bankside outlet will push the hull one way or the other.

Against these forces you can marshal a few of your own. Needless to say, the thrust of the engine is the most powerful. With an outboard or outdrive, this can be directed pretty much as you wish; with an inboard installation you will have to use the medium of a rudder to convert the forward or reverse thrust of the engine into sideways thrust — an altogether less efficient method, but it has the advantage of continuing to work after the propeller has stopped turning, unlike outdrive or outboard steering.

Although an inboard engine basically gives you forward or astern thrust, there is a phenomenon called paddlewheel effect which provides a certain amount of transverse (sideways) thrust at the same time. All engines, even small outboards, produce this thrust, whose effect is greatest just as the propeller begins to turn, and it can be used to advantage when coming alongside or leaving a berth. See Figure 6.1.

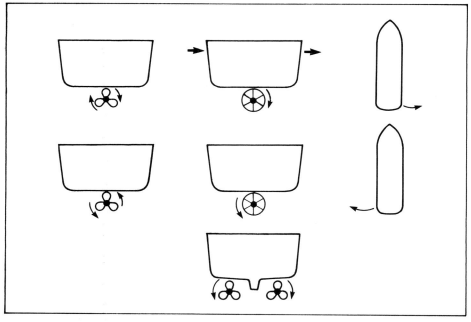

Figure 6.1. *Paddlewheel effect. As a propeller turns it tries to claw its way through the water, but not all of the thrust is forwards. There is a sideways component which acts at right angles to the direction of travel. This transverse thrust or 'paddlewheel effect' is greatest when the propeller starts to turn, and can be used to advantage in manoeuvring. The effect can be most easily visualized if you imagine a paddlewheel turning in place of and in the same direction as the propeller. With the propeller/wheel turning clockwise, transverse thrust acts to port and the stern of the boat is given a kick to starboard.*

Most propellers on single-engined boats are right-handed; that is to say, they turn clockwise when going ahead, anticlockwise when going astern. Left-handed propellers are found on twin-engined craft, usually on the port side so that the two props are 'outward-turning' and each one's paddlewheel effect cancels the other's out (bottom diagram).

The top diagrams show the effect with a right-handed propeller turning ahead, or a left-hander turning astern. The centre diagrams show a right-hander turning astern or a left-hander turning ahead. If you want to give the stern of a single-engined boat with a right-handed prop a kick to starboard (for example, when mooring starboard-side-to), select forward gear and blip the throttle momentarily. The boat will hardly move forward at all; most of the thrust will be sideways, and

the stern will be pushed to starboard. If you wanted to bring the stern to port, you would need to select astern gear.

With a twin-engined boat (bottom diagram) the two propellers are offset from the centreline and offer much improved manoeuvrability anyway, but you can still use the paddlewheel effect. In the more usual case of outward-turning props, ahead on port and astern on starboard will bring the stern to port; astern on port and ahead on starboard will bring the stern to starboard.

Not to be discounted is the effect of inertia on your manoeuvring. As Newton proved, a body at rest will remain at rest and a body in motion will continue in motion until acted on by an external force, and it takes a pretty substantial external force to alter the state of a 5- to 10-ton boat. If you forget about inertia, the manoeuvre may go disastrously wrong; remember it, and its effect too can be used to your advantage.

Finally, there is the possibility of your using external forces of your own. Mooring lines and anchor warps can be used either to hold or to pull bow or stern in the direction you require. Boathooks can be used to push the boat away from the quay (but never to fend off, which is a job for squashy fenders).

GETTING CLEAR

The first thing to do before you cast off is therefore to check on the forces acting on the boat. Which way will the wind try to push you? If you are moored behind the shelter of another craft, as your bow noses out it will be caught by the wind, so you will need to be ready to apply moderate helm in the opposite direction – if the wind is to port, stand by to apply port helm, and vice versa.

If you are moored alongside with the wind blowing from the near bank, the task of casting off will be much easier. With the wind blowing across the cut, pushing you into the bank, you will have to overcome its effect before you go anywhere.

Is there a current? If so, can it be used to your advantage? Current can be deceptive. It will not necessarily go downstream. Near the banks of rivers there is often a counter-current that flows in the opposite direction to the main stream. Watch the movement of floating sticks or leaves for an indication of how this may affect you when you get under way.

You cannot afford to lose control of the boat when leaving a berth, especially if you have to extricate yourself from a line of other moored craft. Facing upstream and with negligible wind, you can push the bow off and apply helm in the same direction. The combination of helm and current will swing the bow towards the middle of the river, and you can then engage forward gear and pull clear. Watch your stern to make sure it does not clout the quay or the next boat in line.

You can use the same technique on a canal with no current but a wind blowing along the cut. Bear in mind, however, that without the current – that is, with no water flowing past the rudder – you will not get steerage until you are properly under way.

Less straightforward cases will require the use of one of your mooring lines as a 'spring', to hold bow or stern near the quay while you use the engine to pull the opposite end of the boat clear. If possible the spring should start off as a breast rope – in other words, should lie perpendicular to the quay – and must, under all circumstances, be run back aboard the boat so that it can be released from on board.

Often it is best to come out stern first, with a spring from the bow and your engine pulling you out from the bank: if you try coming out ahead, your stern may bump along the quay and your bow end up scraping along the boat in front.

You should keep all available fenders over the side when mooring up or leaving a berth, and if you can spare the manpower have one of your crew hold a 'roving fender' which can be moved along the hull to points of likely contact. Never allow your crew to use hands, feet or boathooks to fend off: the first two break and the third can put out an eye or a window.

All manoeuvring of a boat should be carried out with the minimum of engine power. A crash stop, with engine or engines going full astern, is noisy, unpredictable in its effects and usually unnecessary: gentle movements of the throttle are all that should be needed, and if you have to go full astern you were travelling far too fast.

Remember the paddlewheel effect, which will tend to push your stern sideways. If you have a single-engined boat with the more normal right-handed propeller, the effect will work to your benefit if you go ahead leaving port-side-to berths and go astern leaving starboard-side-to berths.

STEERING

A boat is steered using either a rudder or the propeller itself, operated via a tiller or a wheel. Wheel steering is the simpler to understand: if you want to turn to port – that is, left – you put your left hand down so that the wheel turns anticlockwise. For a starboard turn it is right hand down. In other words, the wheel operates in the same way as the steering wheel on a car.

Tiller steering takes a bit more getting used to, because although it is much more positive than wheel steering it appears at first to be contradictory: if you want to turn to port, you push the tiller over to starboard, and vice versa. This is because the bar of the tiller is invariably on the opposite side of its pivot point from the rudder, so that when the tiller goes to starboard, the rudder turns to port. If you are not sure of the effect, imagine it viewed from above: with the tiller over to port and the rudder over to starboard, the angle the rudder makes with the boat can be treated as part of a circle, and the boat will turn along the circumference of that circle.

Every craft responds differently to movements of the helm, depending on the size and type of rudder or drive, the underwater hull shape and the distribution of weight in the hull. So the first thing you have to do after clearing the berth in an unfamiliar boat is to familiarize yourself with its handling characteristics.

Despite the variety of designs, there are some basic rules common to all types of boat. After an initial hesitation (see Figure 6.2) the bow will continue to swing in the required direction all the time that helm is

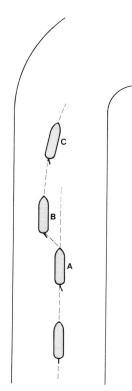

Figure 6.2. *Carry. A boat does not respond instantly to movements of the rudder. If you are travelling in a straight line and put the helm over to starboard (A), there will be a short period of 'carry' during which nothing happens. Then (B) the whole will move, not to starboard, but to port. It will still face in the same direction and follow a track parallel to its old track. The longer the boat is, the more pronounced and protracted this effect will be – the illustration shows a grossly exaggerated example for reasons of clarity. Finally the bow will start to swing to starboard and the turn you wanted will begin (C).*

applied. As the boat comes on to the right heading, you therefore need to stop it turning. Experts will centre the helm a couple of seconds early so that the rate of turn slows and the boat stops turning altogether exactly on cue, but this takes some practice and at first you will have to counter the swing with a small amount of opposite helm. A few degrees will suffice; if you overdo the correction, the bow will start to swing back in the opposite direction and you will end up weaving all over the river.

Another basic rule is to use the minimum amount of helm possible at all times. There should be no need to put the helm hard-a-starboard or hard-a-port except when berthing, clearing a berth or in an emergency. Full-rudder turns can disorientate you, so that you allow the boat to swing too far and miss your heading. If you want to alter course rapidly, it is easier to apply moderate helm and give the throttle a short blip as you do so; this will increase the water flow past the rudder and speed up your rate of turn without increasing the speed of the boat. With outboards and outdrives, you should apply helm first, then power, for the best effect.

Steering would be a lot simpler if in a turn to starboard the part of the boat ahead of the helmsman swung to starboard, while the part astern of him swung to port. Unfortunately, it does not always work like that. A boat will turn about a pivot point somewhere along its centreline, and this may be a long way from the helm. Going ahead, the pivot point will be in the forepart of the hull, so that in a turn the stern skids round and describes a larger arc than the bow (see Figure 6.3). If the helmsman is right at the stern, as is the case on a narrowboat, the swing will appear to be much more dramatic than it actually is. On a cruiser, where the helm is likely to be nearer amidships, the effect will be less noticeable.

It is important to identify this pivot point because with a long boat and a narrow opening such as a bridge arch the 'skid' has to be controlled very accurately if you want to avoid scraping the sides as the stern passes through the opening. Turning astern, the pivot point moves aft, making life easier for the narrowboat helmsman but more difficult for the centrally placed cruiser helmsman.

While on the subject of going astern, it is worth perhaps risking being accused of stating the obvious: that boats are designed to go ahead and so are less easily controllable when going astern. This is especially true in a strong wind, where as you go astern and the pivot point moves aft the boat tends to act as a giant weather vane, turning its stern to the wind and keeping it there. This, known in fact as 'weathercocking', is almost impossible to avoid. If you cannot complete the turn by going forward, you may have to pole yourself round or even drop an anchor (see 'Anchoring' later in this chapter).

Twin engines improve manoeuvrability enormously. They are mounted not centrally, but a couple of feet to one side of the centreline; if you shift the starboard engine into neutral and apply starboard helm, the port engine will act as a lever, giving a much tighter turn than

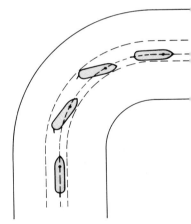

Figure 6.3. *Pivot point. A boat does not follow a neat curve as it turns. It will tend to turn around a pivot point somewhere forward of amidships, with the result that the bow describes a smaller circle than the stern and the hull 'skids' round. Going astern, the opposite happens: the pivot point moves aft and the stern describes the smaller circle.*

would be possible with a single-engined craft. You can improve the rate of turn yet further by running the starboard engine astern at the same time, which will allow you to turn within your own length.

Talk of turning leads on to the problem of turning round in a canal. A three-point turn is not possible when the boat is 50 feet long and the cut is only 45 feet at its widest, so most canals have occasional 'winding holes' where with a certain amount of backing and filling even a 70-footer can be turned through 180 degrees. If you can, send someone ashore with a sternline on the opposite side of the canal from the winding hole; then nose gently into the hole and use a combination of astern thrust, rudder and the crew pulling on the sternline to pull your stern back into the channel to face in the required direction. If you cannot get someone ashore, you may need to pole your way round, as winding holes are often clogged with weed and reed.

The easiest place to turn round in, incidentally, is not a winding hole but a canal junction. A winding hole will often involve you in a five-point or even seven-point turn if you cannot get someone ashore; at a junction you can invariably achieve a full 180-degree turn in three.

Full-length narrowboats can only be turned round at junctions or in 'winding holes'. In strong winds it may be necessary to get a line ashore to help pull the stern round.

RULE OF THE ROAD

Although boats are subject to fewer restricting regulations than any other form of transport, there is a Rule of the Road which is a mixture of statutory obligation, convention and common sense. The Rule (or rather set of rules) deserves to be learnt and adhered to, in the interests not only of your own safety and that of other waterways users, but also of the waterways themselves. Travelling at over the speed limit on canals, for example, will break down the banks, which means that the British Waterways Board or appropriate authority will have to divert precious resources from rebuilding tunnels and locks of closed waterways to strengthening banks of open ones. You know it makes sense!

The most important rules are:

■ Keep to the right when passing other craft. It is a good idea to drive on the right even on a deserted waterway, so that you are not taken by surprise when other craft appear. Bear in mind that not everyone will stick to this rule all the time, especially when rounding bends: the deepest water is usually to be found on the outside and therefore most boats will take the outer bank irrespective of whether it is on their right or left. The risk is not so much of grounding, but of loss of manoeuvrability in the shallows.

■ Give way to any craft that you are overtaking. The normal procedure is to overtake to port.

■ When travelling upstream on rivers, give way to craft coming downstream. Although this might seem unfair, since the other boat has the current in its favour and you are having to work for every yard, it is perfectly logical, because you have much more room to manoeuvre. You have the option of slowing down so that you are barely stemming the current, yet still retain steerage way; if the other boat stops dead, losing all steerage, it will still be travelling downstream at the speed of the current, and the helmsman will have no means of controlling the boat.

■ Give way to all sailing craft when they are travelling under sail alone (when they have an engine running, even if it is only as an auxiliary, they count as being under power and are subject to the same rules as powered craft). This can be somewhat irritating, especially when you turn a corner of a river to see a fleet of racing dinghies bearing down on you. They will often be tacking to and fro, forming an apparently impenetrable wall from one bank to the other: all you can do is slow down and thread your way through, trying to head round their sterns rather than cutting across their bows.

■ Keep out of the way of commercial craft. This is as much a matter of self-interest as anything else, since they will usually be larger than your boat, but they may also have to keep within a more restricted channel than you.

■ Never overtake a commercial vessel when approaching a lock. The skipper has a living to earn, and the time he spends waiting for you to lock through is money lost. If there is a lock-keeper, he will rightly give the working boat priority.

■ Never exceed the speed limit. On the narrow canals your speed will be limited to 4mph, or less – if you find that your boat is creating a 'breaking wash' at this speed, slow down. A wash that forms a foaming breaker on top will suck at the bank, gradually eroding it. The closer you are to the bank, the slower the speed at which your wash will cause damage.

On other canals and on rivers the speed limit will be greater, up to about 7mph in some cases. Make sure you know the limit before you venture afloat, but again do not go by the letter of the law: watch the bank and moored boats to ensure that you are not disturbing either.

You may come across a speed limit marked in knots. A knot is one nautical mile per hour, or 1.15 statute miles per hour: thus a speed of 3 knots is roughly equivalent to about 3½mph, 6 knots equivalent to 7mph.

■ Do not overtake in a lock cut, narrow fairway or anywhere else where navigation is restricted.

■ Sound your horn when approaching blind bends.

■ Only moor overnight where you will not cause an obstruction – never in or near bridgeholes or locks, or on bends.

■ Never throw rubbish over the side.

GRINDING TO A HALT

You may find as you travel along that you suddenly lose steerage. This often indicates that you are aground, or that the water is so shallow that your hull is grinding along the bottom. Water supply is critical on many canals, and depths are uneven, especially in short pounds – the stretches between the locks – and underneath bridges, where local vandals have a distressing tendency to chuck bricks, stones and other rubbish.

If you hit bottom going ahead, the chances are that it will be your bow that goes aground. Try backing off, and if that does not work call the crew aft to raise the bow. Poling off, or sending the crew ashore with lines if this is possible, may also help.

Bridgehole obstructions can often be removed, as long as you have someone on board prepared to strip down to swimsuit and boots and brave the shallow but muddy water. Washing machines and prams are relatively easy to shift provided they have not been there for long, but where someone has been demolishing the bridge coping and dropping the rubble into the cut, the job of clearing it may take some time.

An extended stretch of shallows is a more intractable problem. You could try redistributing the weight to reduce draught to a minimum, and again sending the crew ashore – though bear in mind that you might not be able to get them back on board if you travel only a few yards before becoming stuck again – but often there will be no other

OPPOSITE
Figure 6.4. *Coming alongside. The procedure for coming alongside demands accurate timing and good co-operation between helmsman and crew. Do the right thing too late and it will have the opposite effect from the one you want. Where there is a current, always approach the mooring from downstream if possible: this enables you to retain steerage way even when making no way over the ground, as water will still be passing the rudder.*

Approach very slowly and at an angle of 25–30 degrees to the bank, putting the helm over only in the last few yards and blipping the throttle to give the rudder added effect. It is easier to berth port-side-to in a single-engined craft, because as you go astern to stop the boat the paddlewheel effect brings the stern into the quay. When the bow is almost touching the quay (A₁), centre the helm again and apply gentle revs astern. There should be no need to go full astern; if you do have to, you recourse but to sit and wait until the level in the cut has built up again. Each time a lock is used above you the water will get a little deeper. Unfortunately, it also works in reverse: each time a lock below you is used, the level in your pound will fall. It may be worth sending someone along the towpath to dissuade anyone hoping to come up to your level from doing so.

Another possible reason for losing steerage is a fouled propeller. Weed, rope or plastic bags can all effectively immobilize a prop. Outboards and outdrives are easy to free, as they can be tilted clear of the water and the obstruction removed with a sharp knife (a breadknife or other serrated blade is ideal).

The propellers of inboard-engined craft are less accessible, as they lie directly underneath the boat and cannot be reached from outside without someone diving under the surface. The hull should have a weed hatch, a cut-out in the bottom plating to which is bonded a vertical tube with its top lip above the surface. If you remove the lid of the tube – usually a matter of undoing a single wingnut – you can reach all the way down to the prop to clear it.

ANCHORING

Inland waterways craft do not need the substantial ground tackle of their coastal equivalents, but they do need at least an anchor or a mudweight permanently coupled to a strong line. The anchor or weight should be available for immediate use; if the engine fails opposite the entrance to a weir stream, you will need to be able to stop first and think afterwards.

Anchors can sometimes be used to help in tricky unberthing situations, such as in an onshore wind, as long as you think ahead when you moor up. If you drop anchor 10 yards out from the quay and pay out line as you approach the berth, you will have a ready-made means of pulling yourself clear when it is time to leave. If you do this, make sure that the anchor line is weighted so that it lies along the bottom and does not risk fouling the propellers of other craft.

MOORING

Coming into a berth is much easier than leaving one, because once you have lines ashore you can use them to position the boat as required. If possible, you should approach from downstream because you can then retain steerage way even when the boat is stopped relative to the quay.

Because of the paddlewheel effect it will be easier to moor port side to with a boat with right-handed propeller, when going astern will tuck your stern in neatly (see Figure 6.4). This should not, however, influence your choice of which side to moor, since the same effect will work to your disadvantage when you leave; what you gain on the swings, etc.

Figure 6.4 contd.
must have been approaching far too fast. If carried out properly, the exercise will end with the boat stopped, alongside and parallel with the quay (A_2). The crew can then step ashore with the lines.

When berthing starboard-side-to, approach at no more than 10–15 degrees to the quay (B_1). Put the helm over on your final approach as before, but avoid going astern. Instead, approach the quay even more slowly, with the engine idling in neutral; keep the rudder on all the way in. If you were to go astern at this point, you would find that the stern would kick to port, which you do not want, so as the bow reaches the quay get your crew over the side fast. You will still be moving ahead slowly, but as long as you have not misjudged the speed or angle you will be travelling parallel to and alongside the quay (B_2). With the crew ashore, a combination of astern gear and lines can be used to bring the boat to a halt.

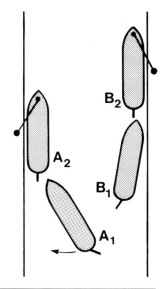

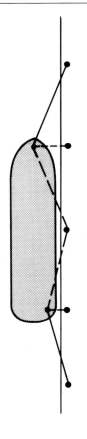

Figure 6.5. *Making fast. How many lines you use to moor your boat will depend very much on the prevailing conditions. Where there is a high wind, strong current or the possibility of large vessels passing close by, up to six lines can be put out – a bowline and a sternline (shown solid in the diagram), two breastlines (dotted, perpendicular to the quay) and two springs (dotted, at an angle to the quay), although breastlines should not be used where there is rise and fall of tide. On a canal in calm conditions just a bowline and a sternline may be all that is required; a spring can be very useful, however, when you need to leave a tight berth.*

Choose a mooring spot that gives you the maximum length of clear bank, without projections, and watch especially for shallows and stakes or other obstructions. You should approach slowly, at a relatively shallow but constant angle: do not try running parallel to the next boat along and then nipping in once you are past it – while this technique may work with cars, it never does with boats.

As you approach, your crew should be ready on the foredeck with a coiled line whose other end is firmly secured to a cleat (there are few things funnier than the sight of a crew landing on the quay with a line that is not made fast to the boat). Get a line ashore as soon as you can, but do not expect your crew to jump across a 6-foot gap.

Once ashore, the bowline can be used to bring the boat to a complete halt if the engine has not already done so. The angle the line makes with the quay should be as shallow as possible to prevent the stern swinging out as the bow is drawn in. Running a sternline ashore at the earliest opportunity will help.

The standard arrangement of lines gives a bowline leading forward from the bow and a sternline leading aft from the quarter nearest the bank (see Figure 6.5). This holds the boat securely, but still allows some movement fore-and-aft. It is generally preferred to the alternative of two breastlines (leading from the same points, but perpendicular to the quay), which restricts movement to an uncomfortable roll. For obvious reasons, breastlines should never be used where there is any rise or fall in water levels. To reduce surging when other craft pass by close to, the bowline and sternline can be supplemented with a pair of springs running from the bow aft and from the stern forward.

Knowledge of a few basic knots is essential for anyone who ever handles ropes, and the crew should practise at least the bowline and the round turn and two half-hitches (see Figure 6.6) until they can literally do them with their eyes closed.

You are allowed to moor overnight virtually anywhere on the canal system, except on private property or where it would be dangerous to do so – such as in locks, bridgeholes or on blind bends. If possible, you should avoid the towpath side, unless it puts you over the wrong side of the cut from civilization (pubs and shops). Where there are no rings or bollards to tie up to, mooring stakes have to be used. These are metal rods about 18 inches long which you have to hammer into the bank. Angle them so that they are pointing away from the direction of strain, and if you do moor on the towpath side of the canal make sure that your lines do not cross the path or the stakes present a danger to pedestrians.

If you have to moor alongside another boat, convention – and enlightened self-interest – dictate that you should not rely on its lines for your security. Take your own lines ashore, and put out plenty of fenders. Two more conventions of lying alongside are worth noting: always ask for permission first unless there is no one on board the other craft; and to get ashore, cross their foredeck rather than their stern.

Figure 6.6. *Knots. If a moored boat is to stay moored, its lines should be secured with knots that are easy and quick to make, will not jam and yet can be relied upon not to come undone of their own accord. There are half a dozen knots which will cover most applications, and time spent teaching the crew how to do them will save time later when mooring or leaving a berth.*

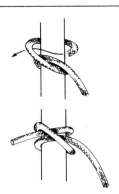

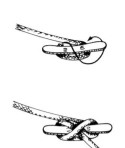

The bowline gives you a ready-made loop that you can drop over mooring bollards. It is totally secure, will not work loose if untensioned, will not jam and can always be undone, no matter how much tension has been applied. If your crew learns only two knots, make this one of them.

If you make up the two half-hitches of the previous knot around something solid such as a guardrail, they form a clove hitch. This is useful for securing lanyards (the lines of fenders and other small items), but it can work loose if the line is not kept taut – on a fender, the strain is provided by gravity.

The reef knot is used for joining two ends of the same rope or two lines of the same type and thickness, when both are under tension. It should not be confused with the quite useless granny knot, and one way of ensuring you get a reef knot is to remember to make it 'right over left and twist; left over right and twist'.

Securing a line to a cleat is called 'making up' a line. There is no need for more turns on the cleat than are shown here, but note that the procedure starts with a full clockwise turn round the base, followed by a figure of eight and a half-hitch – a final turn twisted through 180 degrees before the line is placed over the 'horn' of the cleat – to secure it.

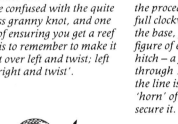

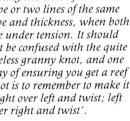

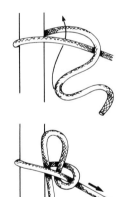

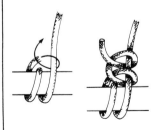

And this is the other: the round turn and two half-hitches. Ideal for securing a line to a ring, eyebolt, or even something as large as a pile, it too needs no tension to keep it intact and yet can be released easily even when under load.

A slippery hitch is the ultimate instant-release knot; it requires just a single tug on the tail to undo. Like the clove hitch, it should never be used to secure an untensioned line, but it provides an effective means of temporarily attaching fenders to a guardrail.

Dissimilar sizes or types of rope can be joined with a sheet bend. In this the thinner or more pliable line (shown cross-hatched in the diagram) nips itself against the more solid rope. Again, both ropes should be kept under tension.

Should you be unfriendly enough to want to dissuade anyone else from lying alongside, you could always hang some nappies out to dry. Don't expect it to work, though: most experienced boaters are wise to that particular wrinkle.

LOCKS

That great invention of Leonardo da Vinci, the mitre lock, is still with us today, and though there are different varieties of lock on different rivers and canals, their principle of operation remains the same. For the most part you will have to open and close them yourself – which is part of the fun of a cruising holiday – but on bigger rivers such as the Thames and Trent and on some commercial waterways there are lock-keepers who will do it for you.

Mitre locks have gates which when closed form a chevron pointing towards the upper level. This ensures that when the levels on each side of the gates are different, the greater pressure on the upper side pushes against the gates and keeps them firmly closed.

The gates will each have a balance beam, roughly the same length as the gate itself, which can be used to push them open when the level of water on each side is equal. Although it will be possible to open the gates against a modest difference in levels, don't: it puts unnecessary strain on the balance beam, the hinges and the gate itself. Similarly, never use the bow of the boat to nose the gates open. Convenient it may be, but it does the gates no good at all.

Each lock normally has four gates, but there are a number of exceptions to this general rule. In the interests of water conservation, some waterways with large locks have an intermediate pair of gates part-way along each chamber so that when a shorter boat locks through, the entire lock chamber does not have to be filled or emptied.

Mitre gates are by no means universal. On many narrow canals the locks have only one pair of mitre gates, at the lower end of the chamber, with a single gate hinged to open uphill at the top; some others have a single gate at each end. Another exception is to be found on the East Anglian rivers. On the Great Ouse the top pair of gates is replaced by a single guillotine gate which is raised so that a boat entering or leaving the chamber can pass underneath. On the River Nene the bottom gates are guillotines.

There is one more exception. A series of locks is called a 'flight', the stretches of water between them 'pounds'. (This is how pound locks got their name; 'pound' used to be the term for the stretch between each pair of gates, the bit that we now call the chamber.) On some steeper inclines the canal builders used to do away with pounds altogether, so that the top gates of one lock formed the bottom gates of the next and so on, making a staircase of locks with up to ten chambers. One of the best known of these is the Foxton flight on the Leicester arm of the Grand Union, which consists of two five-lock staircases in succession.

*Drawing the top gate paddles
at a single-gate narrow lock.*

Hydraulic paddle gear – less attractive than the rack-and-pinion sort, but demanding much less effort.

Back to the gates themselves. Since they cannot be opened until the water level is the same on each side, there has to be a separate set of mini-gates, or sluices, to let the water through. These sluices are either cut in the gates themselves or built into the lock walls, with an inlet above the gates and an outlet feeding into the chamber below.

Each sluice has a 'paddle' which can be raised to let the water through and lowered to hold it back. In the traditional gate the paddle is operated manually by rack-and-pinion lifting gear, but at some locks this has now been replaced by hydraulic gear – which demands much less effort but does not quite have the character of the old machinery.

Whatever type of gear a lock has, to raise ('draw') or lower paddles you need a handle called a windlass, which should be carried on board the boat. Make sure that you have the right type for the waterway you are on – there is a 'standard' type, but there are at least three other varieties in use in Britain, not counting the 'spike' unique to the locks of the Calder & Hebble in Yorkshire. The controlling authority (see page 26) will tell you which variety is needed for the locks of a particular waterway.

With rack-and-pinion lifting gear the windlass is inserted on to the shank of the gear and turned so that the pawl which prevents the raised paddle from dropping can be lifted. Although you can raise a paddle with the pawl in place, you should not do so as it will clatter noisily over the teeth of the ratchet, wearing them down.

Once the ratchet has been released you can draw or lower the paddle as appropriate; clockwise to raise, anticlockwise to lower. The rack is directly connected to the paddle, so the length of rack showing above the pinion is a clear indication of whether the paddle is open or closed. When the paddle is fully raised, flip the pawl over the ratchet again.

When lowering, resist the temptation to let the paddle drop of its own accord – not only could this smash the gear, but the spinning windlass could break your wrist. Windlasses should never be left on the gear when the paddles are drawn; if the pawl slips and the paddle drops, the windlass could fly off and hurt someone.

Hydraulic lifting gear still has to be cranked up and down using the windlass, but requires much less effort. In the absence of a rack it has an open/closed indicator in the form of a little tab that moves up and down a slot as the paddle is raised or lowered.

LEFT *Unusual paddle gear on the Calder & Hebble Canal, operated by a 'handspike'.*

RIGHT *The Leeds & Liverpool Canal also has its own paddle gear system, secured by a special 'padlock'.*

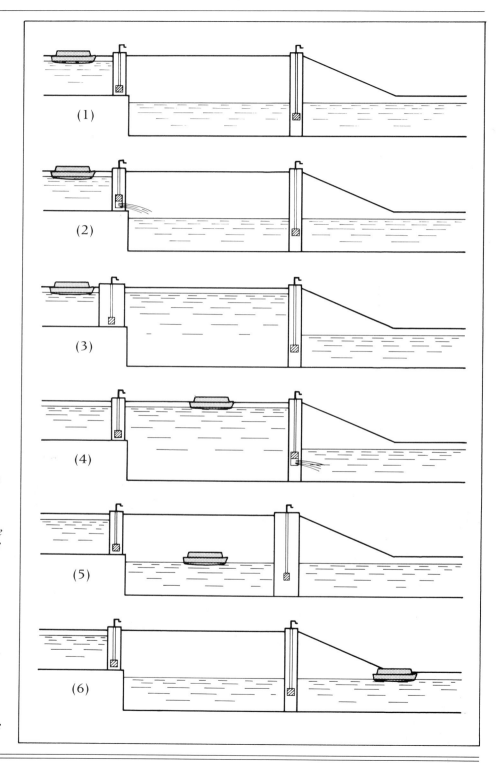

Figure 6.7. *Locking downhill.*
1. Boat arrives at top gates. Check that bottom gates and paddles are closed.
2. (If lock is empty.) Raise top paddles. Where ground paddles are fitted, open these first and wait till the water level in the lock covers the gate sluices before opening the gate paddles.
3. When lock is full, close top gate/ground paddles, open top gates, and enter lock chamber.
4. Open bottom gate paddles, ground paddles first if fitted.
5. When lock is empty, close bottom gate/ground paddles, open bottom gates.
6. Leave lock chamber, and close gates behind you unless there is another craft approaching from the opposite direction.

The sequence of operations descending a lock is illustrated in Figure 6.7, which shows a single chamber with gate paddles. With ground paddles the sequence will be the same, but the mechanism will be on the lockside, not fixed to the gates. Some locks have both gate and ground paddles, in which case the ground paddles should be drawn first, the gate paddles only when their outlets are underwater.

Every time you pass through a lock a chamberful of water escapes with you from the upper to the lower pound. The most economical use of water is achieved when up-bound and down-bound traffic take it in turns to lock through, so that the descent of one boat is followed by the ascent of another. This is not always practical, especially on staircase flights, but if you arrive at a lock that is against you – that is, with the chamber filled if you want to ascend – and can see a boat approaching from the opposite direction, do wait for it. Water is too precious on our canal network to waste.

Some locks have side ponds. These are designed to save water, and should be used where available, as each locking-through in such a case loses only half a chamberful to the lower pound. The procedure involves filling the lock from (or emptying it into) the side pond until the levels in the pond and the chamber are the same, then using the gate or ground paddles to complete the emptying or filling of the chamber in the usual way. A variation on this theme is found on some canals with interconnected pairs of narrow locks, where one is used as a side pond for the other.

Most locks have laybys on both uphill and downhill sides, and there are sometimes piles to which you can moor temporarily while waiting.

Waiting for a lock – temporary moorings are usually available either on the bank or at special 'walings' such as these just outside the chamber.

On approaching a closed lock, you should tie up and send someone ashore to check whether the lock is being used or whether another boat is approaching from the opposite direction. If the lock is open, go straight in unless a lock-keeper directs you to wait – he may be expecting a commercial customer who gets priority.

When entering a lock to descend, make sure that you go far enough in to clear the sill which projects several feet into the chamber from the foot of the top gates. As the chamber empties, this sill may be uncovered and if your stern happens to be just above it you could severely damage your sterngear – or suddenly find the stern 3 feet higher than the bow, with disastrous consequences.

Entering a narrow lock with a narrowboat could not be easier, as the boat fills the width of the chamber and will almost direct itself in. Once in, although you can get away without putting out any lines, it is a good idea to send at least a sternline ashore to your crew, who can then take a turn round a bollard and use the line to halt the boat. The boat will surge back and forth as the lock fills, but this can be controlled with short bursts of engine power.

In wider locks you will have to use lines to hold the boat while the chamber fills or empties. These should never be secured on the lockside, but should be held by your crew with a turn around the bollard. The crew can then haul in or pay out line as the boat rises or falls.

Beware of the sill. The base for the top gates of many locks extends 3 feet or more into the chamber. If your bow (or worse, your stern) is above the sill when the chamber is emptied, it may settle on the sill – with disastrous results.

If there is a lock-keeper, he will usually tell you whether to lie to port or starboard in a wide chamber. At an unmanned lock you will have to decide for yourself, and if you are sharing the lock with another boat the convention is for the first one in to indicate to the other how to lie.

This brings us on to the need for crew. Although you can work unmanned locks with just a pair of adults, operating the paddles and gates is hard graft and the more musclepower you have the better. Any children in your crew can be co-opted to help – indeed, they may insist on helping for as long as it takes to get tired or bored – but may slow up proceedings, which will make you unpopular with anyone who is waiting to use the lock after you. As a general rule a complement of three adults or teenagers is a comfortable minimum if you are on a waterway with a fair number of unmanned locks. If while waiting your turn at the lock you notice that the boat in front of you has a short-handed crew, do give them a hand – not only as a matter of courtesy, but out of self-interest as well, since it will help speed up your passage through. Before leaving a lock you should always make sure that all paddles are fully closed. Again, this is not just a courtesy to the next user, but a sensible precaution against water loss. You may leave the exit gates open unless the other pair is leaking, in which case both pairs should be left closed.

BRIDGES

By far the majority of bridges on our waterways system are fixed (see Chapter 10), but in some areas where it was impractical to build a full-height bridge you will come across opening ones. Manned bridges are rare; they usually work to a published schedule, opening either at specific times or on demand between certain times. You can get details either from one of the waterways guides or from the bridge-keeper.

More common throughout the system are the unmanned opening bridges, which the boater will be expected to operate for himself. There are two basic types, the lifting and the swing or turn bridge. Lack of maintenance sometimes makes them rather stiff to work, but the lifting bridge is counterbalanced and the turn bridge, which remains horizontal but swings across the cut, usually moves easily once you have overcome its initial inertia. You may need a windlass to operate them, in which case it will be the same type as the one used on the locks on that canal.

Bridges, fixed or opening, sometimes provide a useful means of monitoring your progress. It is rare for towns or villages to mark their boundaries with a waterside name board, so faced with the anonymous walls of houses you may find it difficult to tell exactly where you are. Locks will usually be marked with their name or number, but it may be miles between each lock. Bridges are much more common, and on most canals are conveniently numbered in sequence so that, given a guide to the waterway, you can always find yourself on the map.

Farm swing bridge. These often require some effort to get moving, especially on little-used branches.

TUNNELS

Where a canal under construction met a hill, the engineer had three choices: to go round, over or through. If the first two options were impractical, he was faced with the mammoth task of tunnelling through the hill. It must have been a horrific job for the early navigators; even today, with modern machinery, it is pretty unpleasant.

Tunnels are cold, dank, dark and sometimes eerie. But they are also superb engineering achievements, many being well over a mile long, and they have their plusses for the boater: the challenge of working through without once touching the sides and the because-it's-so-nice-when-you-stop type of pleasure – a dim light appears at the end of the tunnel, and grows with infuriating slowness until suddenly you break out into dazzling daylight.

Working through a tunnel requires a raincoat or oilskins, a powerful light and good concentration. A spot or headlight should always be carried. The boat will tend to keep itself clear of the sides, but needs some help from the helmsman. If you meet a boat coming in the opposite direction, ease as far over to the right as you can: two craft

passing very close to one another will exert a mutual attraction which is difficult even for an expert to counteract.

In the days of horse-drawn canal boats, the towpath would usually end at the mouth of the tunnel. The horse would have to be led over the top, while the boat was 'legged' through either by the crew or by 'leggers' hired for the transit. This was hard work and involved the leggers lying on a board, their feet against the sides or roof of the tunnel, and literally walking the boat through. In a few tunnels there were and still are towpaths, but you should dissuade your crew from using them: they are slippery, sometimes crumbling, and it is all too easy to lose your footing in the dark.

Passing in a tunnel. There is usually more room to pass than there first appears, provided you keep close in to your side of the tunnel and the other boat does the same.

7

LIVING ABOARD

In a perfect world, boat designers would be able to draw up an accommodation plan and then create a hull and superstructure into which it would fit. Unfortunately, the true procedure is almost exactly the reverse: because of their need to provide efficient transport that fits the often limited dimensions of the waterways, boats have accommodation that is invariably something of a compromise. How comfortable life aboard is, whether for a weekend or a fortnight, depends to a great degree on the skill of the designer in achieving a workable interior layout within the constraints imposed by length, beam, hull form, air draught, engine position and so on.

Needless to say, some designers achieve better compromises than others. But however well thought-out their creations, they cannot make boats as spacious or space-efficient as homes on dry land. Living aboard therefore takes a certain skill and organization.

Boats are often sold on the basis of accommodation – as a four-berth or six-berth cruiser, for example. Especially at the smaller end of the scale, builders make claims that at best are optimistic and at worst are quite misleading: a 'four-berth' 18-foot trailable weekender will almost always have berths for just two in a little cabin, the other two camping out in the cockpit under a removable canopy. There will be virtually no stowage space, and no separate toilet compartment. If a toilet is fitted, it will probably be under one of the berth cushions, so that going to the loo in the middle of the night can be an event that disrupts the entire crew. There may be a single-burner stove, and a sink with cold water supply from a jerrican that has to be lugged on and off the boat whenever it needs filling.

On a boat of this size it pays to be realistic in one's expectations. Even with only two people aboard the cabin will be cramped, especially in British weather; if the rain starts bucketing down it is best to go ashore. Occasional nights aboard are OK, but more than a weekend and a less-than-stoic crew may begin to mutter darkly about finding somewhere to have a proper wash.

As length increases the size of the accommodation rises in proportion, but it still pays to view claims with caution. At 21 feet, for example, the cockpit berths may have been moved into the cabin, thereby reducing the space available for the toilet, the cooker, the sink and stowage. Still, two of the berths can often be used as temporary stowage, making living aboard a much more practical proposition.

Not until length reaches about 24/25 feet — when the boat is no longer trailable except by Land Rover or lorry — do you get the sort of interior layout that would be comfortable for four adults for a week or more. A narrowboat or narrow cruiser of this size will probably have a separate toilet, a galley area, two permanent berths and two occasional berths created by lowering the saloon table to form a double. Stowage will still be limited, and permanent work surfaces rare.

A common feature of boats at this end of the size scale is dual-purpose design throughout the accommodation. The saloon will double as the night cabin, the table as a berth, the sink top as a galley work surface. This is certainly economical use of space, but it requires a similar versatility on the part of the crew. Bedding has to be tidied away every morning and cannot be got out again until everyone on board is ready to go to bed; clothes have to be stowed — if not in a locker, at least tucked away at the end of a berth with the bedding.

Larger boats of course offer more space, but often more berths as well — which means the convertible dinette can be found on almost any size of craft, so the rule about putting at least the dinette bedding away first remains valid.

The golden rule with any boat is to keep it tidy. This usually comes as a nasty shock to children (like the author's) used to living in bedrooms with toys wall to wall. They might not have the range of toys aboard that they have at home, but it is surprising how far they can spread a week's supply of clothes, books, paper and pencils.

MAKING A MEAL OF IT

However, it is galley duty that invariably causes the greatest upheaval on a small boat. Almost everything else has to stop while meals are being prepared. If the only work surfaces are sink and cooker lids, the chef will have to prepare the food before cooking it; the rest of the crew, meanwhile, sit round the table and try not to get in the way. If the proceedings are not organized properly, tempers can fray and meals take literally hours to cook.

Breakfast is undoubtedly the worst meal to prepare, with everyone on board trying to get up, wash, dress and tidy away the bedding at the same time as the cook does his or her stuff. Other meals will be simpler to prepare, as the cook is likely to be alone in the saloon, with the rest out on deck. If for any reason (such as bad weather) they are inside, they can be of most help by simply remaining seated.

What to eat on board depends to a large extent on the crew's

Galley space, especially worktop area, is never generous. Unless you relish the challenge of ambitious recipes, simplicity should be the order of the day.

preferences, but one fundamental rule is to keep it as simple as possible. Unless you have an undiscovered Escoffier who relishes the challenge of recreating their star recipes in a quarter of the space and with a quarter of the utensils they have at home, choose meals that can either be whipped up in a few minutes or left untended for hours while everyone gets on with the serious business of amusement.

If you have a two-burner cooker with no oven, you are virtually limited to what you can cook and serve up in two pans. Given an oven and another ring, most recipes are possible, but you should bear in mind the complication of dishing up on a small table and washing up in a small sink. There are several books on cooking afloat, but more useful are those offering recipes for one-pot meals or meals for one. You may find that your own general cookery books have suggestions for meals for working couples – that is, ones that can be drummed up quickly on your return from work – which are often ideal.

Convenience foods may be a dirty word in some households, but living afloat often improves the taste of the blandest meals, and you can always make your own additions – such as prawns to a packeted paella, a healthy dollop of red wine to a boeuf bourguignon or cream and wine to a stroganoff. You might even manage to kid the crew that it's all your own work.

Lunch should always involve the minimum of preparation, so that the cook does not spend the nicest part of the day in exile down below. If you don't stop at a waterside pub for lunch, either give the crew sandwiches and soup or – even better – suggest they help themselves to food as and when they want it. Lay out some cheese, cold meats, tomatoes, cucumber, pickles and bread rolls on a tray, and you will satisfy most people; anyone who wants anything more complicated can forage for themselves. Provided they can be relied upon not to leave the galley looking like a bombsite when they have finished, the result should be quite satisfactory for all concerned – everyone gets the size and type of meal they want, at the time they want, and the cook gets a rest.

Supper invariably takes on more importance than lunch on board a boat: once you have tied up for the night there is plenty of time to cook, eat and drink. But even then it is important not to be over-ambitious. Someone always has to wash up.

One way of reducing the washing up is to have a bankside barbecue. Besides adding a delightful flavour to the food, this does away with the need for at least one pan, and can be used to cook either fish or meat. You don't have to find storage space for a messy metal barbecue and a sackful of charcoal; for a couple of pounds you can now buy self-contained disposable barbecue packs consisting of a foil container, grill, charcoal and lighting fluid which work just as well as the real thing.

A note about making drinks on board. Mugs are certainly more convenient than cups and saucers, whether for coffee, tea or soup; as is so often the case afloat, expediency should rule over ceremony. Take care when buying: some plastic mugs can impart an unpleasant flavour to the drink, or – worse – retain the flavour of the last drink they contained, so that you get coffee tasting of soup or tea tasting of coffee. Never fill mugs more than about three-quarters full. It is too easy on a boat, even one that is not moving, to spill drinks as you pass them out on deck.

KEEPING CLEAN

Small boats are not over-generous in their provision of washing facilities; a small sink with cold-water supply only is common, and even on larger craft with central heating and a separate toilet compartment the sink and basin will be somewhat more compact than the ones in your home. The general lack of space on board is one reason for this, but another equally valid reason is water conservation. An average-sized kitchen sink will take over 3 gallons, which would make short work of emptying the water tank. (Surprisingly, even a shower uses less water.)

If you have no hot-water supply, you will have to rely on pans or kettles to provide the water for washing and washing up. By and large, this means that you are limited to a few pints of hot water at a time, and requires a special approach to washing up to make those few pints go further; rinse all the crockery and cutlery in cold water first, using a brush or cloth to get the food off, and then do your hot wash with detergent.

It may be that your boat has a water heating system that works off the engine cooling system. In this case you will get constant hot water while the engine is running and a limited supply after it stops. With this type of system it makes sense to have the crew do their washing and showering while under way so that there is some hot water left for the washing up.

With a constant supply of hot water provided by a separate heating system there will be no need for any of the above considerations, but you should still impress on the crew the need to conserve water if your holiday is not going to be spent stopping at every tap like a dog investigating lamp posts.

Given the usual lack of facilities, washing clothes any bulkier than underwear is impractical aboard most boats. If you have to have a clean shirt every day, pack enough to see you through the holiday (but see Chapter 8, on clothing). Washing nappies, unpleasant even at home, is doubly so on board. Take along a supply of disposables.

Boats with pressurized water systems will have a water pump that turns itself on at regular intervals, even if the taps are not running, to keep the pressure up in the system. So switch the pump off at night or when you go ashore.

When you switch the pump on again, make sure that the taps are all shut. My family and I were once on a boat with a fold-away basin in the toilet. In the middle of the night my young son got up to go to the loo. When he turned on the tap to wash his hands, no water came out, so he just folded the basin up again and went back to bed, leaving the tap still open. In the morning, when I turned the master switch on again, the water began to flow and we had a good few gallons over the floor before anyone realized.

Showers often have their own electric pump, not to supply the water but to take it away afterwards. The pump is fitted·in a sump below the shower tray and discharges the waste overboard, overcoming the problem of the floor being below the waterline. It may be operated by an automatic float switch, or may have to be switched on and off by the user; in the latter case, make sure you turn it off again when you leave or it will burn out.

STOWAGE

There is a variation of Parkinson's Law that applies to stowage on boats: the amount of gear you have on board expands to fill the space available, and a little bit more besides. Put another way: no boat has enough stowage.

You can do little about increasing the amount of stowage in a boat, but you can reduce the amount you bring on board. There is a universal tendency to throw things into the car at the last moment 'just in case', a tendency that should be resisted.

Watch an experienced hirer take over a boat, and you might wonder why he appears to be taking sack after sack of rubbish on board. He's not, of course; it's just that those black plastic sacks are the ideal suitcase for a boat. Not only can you fit a huge amount of clothing, bedding or other gear in them, but when empty they occupy no space at all, unlike a case, which may often take up half the space available in a locker.

If rubbish sacks are beneath your dignity, most chandlers stock a range of sailing bags or holdalls (at around fifty times the price). They, too, fold away to almost nothing. It should not concern you that your clothes might get a little more creased than they would in a suitcase; if it does, you probably have the wrong clothes for a boating holiday.

Stores are another matter. Even if you get a hire operator to provide a starter pack of provisions, you will probably want to bring your own on board. Since the stuff you do not use will have to be taken away again – in my own family's case, it always seems to be at least half – it is best to hang on to the cardboard boxes.

This means finding a place to stow them (not in the bilges, where they will disintegrate and clog the bilge pump); and that in turn means getting small boxes if possible. A box the size of a wine case is about the largest practical size, and if you are lucky enough to find in your local supermarket a series of boxes that will nest one inside the other, go for it.

Again, you can buy a ready-made equivalent in the form of plastic stacking boxes. These are not expensive, and obviate the risk of your stores falling through the soggy bottom of the box and into the drink just at the moment when you are stepping aboard (it happens).

The principle of getting small boxes because they are easier to stow applies throughout the boat. Food lockers are invariably too small, and often awkwardly shaped. If you bring a stock of household basics on board, especially the type that does not like water or damp – flour, salt, and so on – decant them into sealable plastic containers just large enough to take the amount you are likely to need. There is no point in bringing aboard 1lb of flour and taking 15 ounces home with you.

Another advantage of small containers when cruising on more exposed waters such as the Broads or Scottish lochs is that they can be jammed into lockers. Nothing is more irritating than the sound from below of glass jar clinking perpetually against glass jar. If some of the jars are replaced with plastic containers, the containers can keep the glass apart, safe and silent.

It is a good idea to keep a 'dirty locker' for tools, spares, oil, grease, varnish and so on. If there is room, the engine compartment is ideal. Try to avoid stowing gear loose in here; tins can fall into the bilges or lodge against the hot exhaust pipe, with disastrous effects, and tools idly thrown into the compartment will usually make a beeline for moving parts of the engine.

If there is no room in the engine compartment, devote a deck locker to dirty gear, with a separate one for fenders, ropes and other deck gear. Oily fenders will mark your and other boats' topsides, while greasy ropes can be dangerous.

Damp

One problem that will affect stowage in almost all boats is damp. This is by no means confined to bilges. Cooking, washing, gas heating and people themselves all release humidity into the atmosphere, and in a boat that is not very well ventilated there is nowhere for the moisture to go. Even in a warm, dry summer when the windows or ports are left open to get a through draught, not all the moisture will evaporate: it collects in lockers, in fabrics, and in the foam cushions of settees and berths. It is therefore important to empty the lockers periodically, dry them out with a cloth and let the contents stand outside for a breath of fresh air. While the weather holds, take the opportunity too to remove cushions and curtains and give them an airing.

Pots, pans and all the other impedimenta of the cook's trade should ideally be made of aluminium or good stainless steel. Cutlery, too, has to be stainless, or it will last no time at all. Take care when buying, and if possible buy equipment with a lifetime guarantee; of several different grades of stainless steel it is only the better-quality grades that will withstand prolonged exposure to a marine environment.

Mooring alongside other craft is perfectly acceptable – but first get the permission of anyone left on board, and ensure that you are not obstructing the waterway.

As mentioned earlier, gas heaters and cookers release water vapour into the air – almost twice as much water, in fact as the original weight of the gas burnt. They therefore create a warm, damp environment rather than the warm, dry one you need. Electric heating is impractical because of the current required, so if you want to dry a damp boat you will need central heating with its own radiators or, more commonly, a ducted system. In this the heater itself – usually paraffin or diesel-powered – is sited outside the accommodation; combustion takes place outside, and the water vapour-laden exhaust is expelled into the atmosphere, while a separate supply of air is drawn in, heated and ducted through into the cabin.

If you have a persistent problem with damp and a supply of mains electricity available at your mooring, it may be worth investing in a dehumidifier. Drawing little current, this will extract moisture from the air in the boat and, as the air dries, from the furnishings as well. This will keep the damp at bay while the boat is not in use, and ensure that you are not welcomed on your return by that pervasive smell of mildew. Dehumidifiers are not cheap – around £300 each – but you could always share the cost and the equipment with other owners who have the same problem.

THE ENTERTAINMENT GAME

One of the saddest aspects of modern life is that we seem to require constant stimulation if we are not to get bored. Bombarded on all sides by manufactured sights, sounds and tastes, twentieth-century man finds it difficult to switch off and enjoy peace.

Simple pleasures – the feel of the sun on your face, the sound of birds in the trees, the smell of blossoming nature – will soon pall for blasé city dwellers, to be replaced by an intense craving for further amusement.

This is particularly true of children, whose attention span is often no longer than the gaps between the advertisements on television. Long before you lose interest in the natural beauty around you, your child passengers will be looking for something to do, and if not given it can become a real pest. But even adults need to be kept amused, and it is the duty of every skipper to ensure that his charges do not become bored.

It is all too easy, as you sit at the helm absorbed with the control of the boat, to forget that your passengers do not have the same ready-made distraction. At locks it will be all hands on deck, but in between these bursts of frenetic activity? This section looks at some of the ways you can keep the crew amused.

Chores

One of the great misconceptions of our time is that people go on holiday for a rest. The truth is that we tend to do more on holiday, not less: we think nothing of getting up early to pack a picnic, driving 30 or 40 miles to the seaside or into the country, walking another few miles of beach or woodland, and driving back home. It's not a rest we need on holiday; it's a change from the normal routine.

Somehow, even the routine chores take on a different character on board a boat. People who would not dream of either cooking or washing up in a kitchen ashore suddenly make for the galley; people who would not walk a few hundred yards to the shops at home think nothing of a mile hike into the village for milk; children who cannot be bribed to make their beds are happy to tidy their cabins and bunks.

If nothing else, this suggests that for most people any task is better than no task at all. The last thing an unoccupied passenger wants to hear is an airy 'Don't worry about that, darling – I'll do it.' You may think you are doing them a favour. You're not.

Everyone, even small children, should be given something to do – helping with the washing up for the under-sevens . . .

. . . and helping with mooring up for the older ones.

What all this means is that no one should claim exclusive rights to the jobs available. Steering, daily engine checks, cooking, laying the table, washing up and cleaning the boat should be treated as entertainments to be parcelled out and shared round – perhaps on a strict rota basis; some of your charges may complain, but with luck this will be short-lived. The only caveat, perhaps, is that the person or persons who normally do all of these jobs might be required to supervise. There is nothing worse than eggs scrambled by an eager but ignorant seven-year-old.

Taking it in

The above leads us comfortably on to food and drink. It is a pity that it is not really practical – or good for you – to eat and drink all day. Meals, snacks and refreshers are an excellent way of passing the time, and if no one is particularly rushed the whole process from the serving of the first aperitif to the draining of the last wineglass or coffee cup can be stretched to fill more than two hours.

This is especially true of evening meals aboard, where with good company the talk can continue into the night, with no one feeling the need to move as long as there remains something to nibble and something to sip.

Of course, eating aboard does involve buying the meal, cooking it and washing up. There will be times when all this seems too much effort – and equally, if there really is only one person on board who can cook, the person who normally cooks ashore, it is fair to give him or her a break.

On waterways you are spoilt for choice when it comes to eating or drinking ashore. One of the delights of our rivers and canals is the number of watering holes. These are nothing to do with the stuff that your boat floats on, and only rarely will you be able to get a glass of H_2O in them. They are pubs, frequently serving bar snacks and sometimes with restaurants attached. Originally built to serve the navigators' encampments or for the working boatmen who followed, many are real treasures.

On the Broads and some of the bigger rivers and canals – the Thames being particularly good in this respect – the pubs have made an impressive attempt to cater for the new breed of waterways user, with alongside moorings, children's rooms or play areas, and a range of food from the basic to the exotic.

A holiday for the cook as well: the Thames is particularly well endowed with riverside pubs offering food and a place for the children to run around.

The Natural World

We have covered chores and the inner man (or woman, or child); while one person steers, others might be cooking, tidying the boat, washing, eating, drinking or reading; but in a day's cruising there is more than enough time for all of these, and eventually a time will come when the book or the dischcloth goes down and a 'What shall I do now?' expression appears on the face.

Macclesfield Canal milepost. With canal traffic limited to walking pace, passengers who decide to explore the towpath can easily keep up with the boat and hop back on board when they are tired.

One of the most satisfying ways of occupying time is to use the immediate environment to identify and make familiar the unfamiliar. A good nature book introducing you to the flora and fauna of the waterways is therefore a must; so is a book on the architecture of the canal and riverside (see Chapters 9 and 10).

Buy a good pair of binoculars. 'A good pair' does not mean the most powerful you can find, as the higher the magnification, the more difficult it will be to keep a steady picture. More important is the clarity of the glasses, which depends on the quality of the lenses. 7×50, denoting seven times magnification and focal (front) lenses of 50mm in diameter, should be suitable for most purposes.

Armed with book and binoculars, most passengers can be left happily for hours. Children, too, with their zest for learning, will drink in the information and benefit from it.

The passengers need not be confined to the boat, of course. One of the nicest things about canal cruising is that maximum speed is little faster than an average walking pace, so the amateur naturalists can indulge in their nature-spotting while getting some healthy exercise – and burning off excess energy – on the towpath. On rivers the limit is a little higher, so the skipper will either have to dawdle or supply the passengers with bicycles.

Bicycles, incidentally, offer tremendous value for money on boats. Park a pair of bikes on the foredeck and you suddenly have access, not only to the shops and sights by the waterside, but also to those in villages some way from the river or canal. They come in useful, too, if you are in a hurry: your crew can pedal ahead of the boat and open the lock gates in advance of your arrival.

Fishing

Along the banks of every river and canal, at any time of the year, you will see fishermen. It is important to note that there is mutual antipathy between angler and boater; the former's line is chewed up by the latter's propeller, while the latter's attempt to avoid the aforementioned often results in grounding, near misses or actual collisions.

If you want to join the anglers at their sport, this is best left until the boat is stopped and you can fish from the bank. Casting a trolling line from the stern is not advisable as it may be fouled by other boats, or even by your own prop if you suddenly have to go full astern to stop.

Bear in mind that on many waterways, including the BWB network, you will need a licence to fish, either from the boat or from the bank. There is also a close season for coarse fishing from 15 March to 15 June in most areas.

Swimming

Swimming in canals is strictly forbidden, and on rivers it is prudent to obtain local advice before you let yourself or your crew over the side. If you allow the children to go for a swim, make sure that someone stays on board or on the bank and keeps an eye on them all the time; it will only take a second for them to get into difficulties if they meet a strong current or undertow. Above all, never go bathing above a weir or in a lock cut.

Indoor Pursuits

So much for the outdoor entertainment. But what about the times when you are stuck in the cabin listening to the drum of rain against the coachroof? Or when the sun goes down and a chill steals over the landscape, with supper still an hour or two away?

The first and most important thing is to keep a stock of ready-made entertainments on board. Every boat should have a ship's library; this is true even if you have hired the boat only for the week, when you will have to bring your own. A selection of light reading material could include one or more guides to the waterways, a couple of magazines and the colour supplement you never got round to reading last weekend, and perhaps a few novels.

A vital ingredient of a good holiday: plenty of reading matter.

A notepad and pencil will prove useful for the skipper, serving as a rough log and enabling him or her to keep tabs on progress, fuel and water consumption and so on. To curb the pad's tendency to wander, it is worth including a few spares for other members of the crew. Each pad should have a pencil or pen attached to it with a piece of string, again so that the skipper's does not go missing.

One or two packs of cards and a board game such as Scrabble are a good idea for passing time. Travel Scrabble takes up little space and will not be ruined if you lose one or two tiles, unlike some board games.

Radio and Television

Broadcasting offers ready-packaged entertainment, and unless you are determined to cut yourself off from all news of the outside world on your holiday, a small radio is invaluable. It should have its own batteries; one that has to be plugged in to the boat's electricity supply is less portable, with the result that you may have to turn the volume up to hear it from where you are sitting.

Certain frequencies of sound travel a surprisingly long distance over water, and it is a well-known paradox that music played almost too low to be heard on board because of the engine noise is perfectly audible 50 yards away. It is unreasonable to expect all other users of the waterways to share your taste in music or broadcasting. Keep the volume well down, and never play the radio outside.

In your travels on our waterways you may be unfortunate enough to come across what appears to be a mobile disco, wandering along to the accompaniment of 50W of eardrum-shattering rock music from a ghetto blaster. You can suggest that the occupants turn the noise down, but if they are insensitive enough to play it so loud in the first place your polite suggestion may go unheeded. If the boat in question happens to be going in your direction, the only thing to do is to tie up for half an hour or so to let them get well ahead.

Remember that the BBC broadcasts on different frequencies. In some parts of the country you may have to retune your radio to a different frequency from the one you are used to in order to get the best reception. Independent local radio – there are about seventy different companies – and the BBC's own thirty local stations are a good source of information about events taking place in the area.

Television is less satisfactory on board boats as it is rarely possible to mount the aerial high enough for good reception. Nevertheless, with a 12V set and a portable aerial you need not go without the great twentieth-century opiate. Don't bother trying to run the TV while going along; not only will interference from the engine play havoc with the picture, but the constant changes of direction as you round bends will mean someone spending all their time on the roof adjusting the aerial.

Broadcast frequencies for television channels vary throughout the country. The BBC produces a useful set of cards detailing the frequencies, and also showing which areas are served by which transmitters. The cards have maps on them which help enormously when adjusting the aerial provided you have a reasonable sense of direction. They are available from the BBC's Engineering Information Department, whose address is given in the Appendix to this book.

Children

Most of the ideas outlined above will be suitable for keeping both adults and children amused, but as any parent will know children's entertainment can turn into a full-time occupation. Aboard a boat, where they cannot simply be told to go out into the garden and play, they remain underfoot until you do something about it.

The problem is most acute with the under-tens. It can bring tears of frustration to the eyes of an adult to find them jumping up, only minutes after being settled down with a book or game, wanting something else to do. The only sanity-preserving solution is to have a ready-made inventory of games and pastimes, so that the moment interest in one palls they can pass on to another.

At the very earliest opportunity children should be encouraged to take a hand in the control of the boat. Given strict supervision, even a five-year-old can steer — some of them remarkably well. Later on, you can teach them rope handling, knot tying and fender work.

Bring a box of favourite toys and books, with perhaps a new toy, puzzle book or game bought specially for the holiday. Toys brought from home should include nothing that is precious, and nothing that comes apart unless it does not matter if you lose a few pieces. Thus jigsaws are out, but Lego in. If you bring anything with a lid, secure it with a rubber band before leaving home.

A couple of pounds spent sensibly in Woolworths or Smiths can be a lifesaver. One very cheap prop that you can supply at the beginning of the holiday is a notebook — an ordinary shorthand pad will do — and a set of crayons or fibre-tip pens for each child. Don't bother getting a children's drawing pad or anything sophisticated like that: the notebook should be bought more for the number of pages per penny than for its decoration. Depending on the age of the child, it can be used as a doodle pad or a diary of the trip, or filled with the lists that children seem to enjoy making: one day birds, the next day trees and the next day D-registration cars on the towpath (with my own family, that one lasted long enough to get one entry).

GETTING IN GEAR

Warm clothing is essential, and not just out of season. Even in summer a cool wind blowing over water can chill a static crew.

There are a lot of strange ideas about what constitutes appropriate boating gear. Gone are the days when blazer, tie and knife-crease trousers were compulsory on the river if you didn't want to look like the hired hand. That style of clothing is now only appropriate when you are trying to cut a dash at one of the more prestigious South Coast or Thames yacht clubs. Otherwise, most of the time and in most places, anything goes — unless you happen to be a hired hand, in which case you'll probably be required to dress in a snowy white boiler suit or

quasi-naval uniform while the owner lounges around in a pair of torn Bermuda shorts.

On boats, clothing should be chosen not for its looks, but for comfort and warmth. Baggy trousers and baggy sweaters for the cold days; shorts and T-shirts for those rare scorchers. Ideally your kit should consist of several different grades of 'topwear' that can be worn one over the other. This is because the number of garments is almost more important than the weight of each one, since the air between them adds another layer of insulation. When it is really cold you can wear a loose sweater over a thinner one, with a shirt over a T-shirt underneath, and peel off a layer at a time as the wind drops and the sun comes out.

Do not be tempted to take too many changes of clothing. Apart from underwear, socks and shirts, none of which takes up much space, there is little that cannot be worn for a week. One spare pair of trousers or jeans and one spare sweater, in case you fall in the water or get drenched by an unexpected downpour, should be enough.

Footwear on boats is somewhat specialized, and this is true even on the most inland of inland waterways. Shoes should have soft soles of rubber or even rope, so that they give grip on a wet surface and do not damage the deck. Sailing shoes, which usually have an intricate, high-grip tread pattern on their soles, are ideal, trainers less so as their uppers get damp and dirty. Leather or composition soles are definitely out.

Boat decks are strewn with hard objects, such as mooring cleats and fairleads, at just the right height to catch your toe. Avoid the temptation to go around barefooted if you possibly can.

One of the pleasures of waterways cruising is that any member of the crew can leave the boat and walk along the towpath for as long as he or she wants. Waterproof boots are therefore a good idea, both to see you through the boggy areas that invariably form on the bank and to protect your ankles and shins from inquiring nettles.

Some sort of rainwear is essential. Even if the steering position of your boat is inside, you may need to operate locks in the rain, and there is nothing worse than being caught unprepared by a thunderstorm as you make your way back from a shopping expedition to a village 2 miles away. Going through tunnels is also a dampening experience for an outside helmsman; whether it is raining outside the tunnel or not, there will nearly always be some water streaming from the roof, and it is quite astonishing how much water can pour on to the boat in the ten minutes or so it takes to negotiate a half-mile tunnel.

The ideal wet-weather gear is a set of oilskins. This is a name dating back a century and more to the time when sailors' waterproofs were coats or capes literally coated with oil to repel water. They were heavy, not very effective, and probably stank to high heaven. Happily the only feature they share with their modern derivatives is the name.

Oilskins are now available in a very wide variety of styles and weights, from slip-on kagoule types in light nylon to heavy-duty suits in exotic fabrics that are claimed to be fully waterproof on the outside, but

Sailing shoes are a good investment, even for inland cruising. Their high-grip soles will keep the wearer upright and on board even on oily or slippery decks.

still allow moisture through from the inside to prevent condensation. For most purposes on inland waterways, the lighter models will be adequate.

Front-opening jackets are better than the smock kind, which have to be pulled over the head – not pleasant when they are wet. A hood will be useful, preferably a fixed one as a detachable hood can never be found when you need it. Both the hood and the waist or hem of the jacket should have drawstrings.

Trousers complete the waterproofing, but do not bother buying chest-high ones. These are very inconvenient to put on and take off, as you have to remove your jacket each time to drop the braces, and they are only of use to the sailing and offshore crowd, who have to sit in pools of water with horizontal rain and spray driving up their legs.

A very useful garment is a thermal-pile jacket, which bridges the gap between oilskins and a sweater. Windproof and warm, it will also keep off light drizzle, though it will eventually absorb persistent rain and then, because of its bulk, take an unconscionable time to dry.

Headgear is definitely optional, but if worn it should be chosen for warmth. A woolly hat is ideal, as it can be pulled down over the ears if necessary and worn underneath a hood. Peaked caps might keep off the rain and sun, but you will have to be prepared for ribald comments from your crew, other boats and people standing watching you as you enter locks. If you then fluff the manoeuvre, they'll die laughing.

Not many small boats have hanging lockers, let alone one for clothes and one for wet-weather gear. Nevertheless, if possible the oilskins should be given a locker of their own so that they can drip dry without soaking everything else in the locker.

SAFETY EQUIPMENT

Every boat large enough to sleep its crew should carry on board certain items of basic safety equipment. On inland waterways craft this need not be anything like as extensive as the inventory required by coastal or offshore cruisers, but the equipment on the list is no less essential.

The trade divides safety gear into primary and secondary safety equipment. Primary safety is all about preventing an emergency. When the primary system fails and an emergency arises, secondary safety equipment swings into action. An example of the former might be a gas detector, of the latter a fire extinguisher: if the detector fails to raise the alarm or shut off the supply, an extinguisher may prove necessary to put out the resultant fire.

Prevention being better than cure, primary safety should be your main concern. This is more a state of mind than anything else: keep children inboard, or where they can be clearly seen; never smoke or brew up while refuelling; never switch on the electricity until you know there has not been a gas leak in your absence.

But however much effort and money you spend on primary safety,

Some type of effective waterproof is important. You never know when you may have to operate locks in the rain.

you cannot assume that nothing will go wrong or that everything will work as nature or the manufacturer intended. Secondary safety equipment is still essential.

Lifejackets

Every child and every non-swimmer aboard a boat should be encouraged to wear a lifejacket or buoyancy aid at all times when on deck, and the boat should carry one for every person on board. Lifejackets are more expensive, but for British Standards approval they have to pass a stringent test that checks their ability to turn an unconscious wearer face-up within five seconds of falling in the water. They are available in various forms, with inherent foam buoyancy, air inflation, air/foam buoyancy (a limited amount of foam that can be topped up with air from a mouthpiece) or gas inflation. The first three are uncomfortably bulky for all-day use, but gas inflation models are no more troublesome than a safety harness. These are worn folded, and are inflated either automatically on immersion or when a pull is operated on the integral CO_2 (carbon dioxide) bottle. Unfortunately, because of the risk of accidental inflation, they are not recommended for children.

All young children should be made to wear a buoyancy aid when on deck or playing about near the water . . . and should be watched to make sure they don't undo it when you are not looking.

Buoyancy Aids

Much more popular with children, and generally cheaper than the lifejacket, is the buoyancy aid. This is a waistcoat-type jacket with inherent foam buoyancy. Depending on the model, they are relatively comfortable and attractive. Their only real drawback is that they are not guaranteed, like the lifejacket, to turn a wearer over without help from him or her.

Harnesses

At the very earliest opportunity children should be taught how to walk round a boat safely, and how to behave in locks. Until that moment arrives, they should be either kept inside or attached to a rail or lifeline with a safety harness. This should have sufficient line to allow them reasonable movement, but not so much that it tangles them up or drags them through the water if they should fall overboard. Five to 6 feet is usually ample. The line should have a carbine hook at the end, a simple but strong hook that can be clipped on to the rail using just one hand and can be released instantly if necessary.

Fire Extinguishers

The greatest hazard on a boat is fire, and with gas and inflammable fuels aboard there is plenty of scope for an accident. Every boat should carry at least two extinguishers in different positions (so that if you are unable to reach one because of the fire you can still get hold of the other).

For general use Halon or BCF extinguishers are best. These release a chemical extinguishant that douses the flames without leaving a mess, unlike the still-common dry-powder extinguisher, and can be used safely on engine-room, galley or electrical fires. They do not, however, cool down the source of the fire, so you have to look out for any signs of spontaneous re-ignition.

Automatic BCF or CO_2 systems are a good idea for engine rooms. These operate of their own accord if the temperature in the compartment rises beyond a certain point, and obviate the need for you to open the hatch to fight the fire yourself (which might cause a 'flashover' that immediately spreads the fire throughout the boat).

Another good idea, for the galley this time, is a fire blanket. These used to be made of asbestos, but now tend to be glass cloth. They work on the same principle as CO_2 extinguishers, by excluding air from the fire, and are ideal for pan fires where an aerosol extinguisher might blow burning droplets out of the pan.

Lifebuoys

Not essential, but valuable if you have the room, is a lifebuoy of either horseshoe or ring shape. It should be kept on deck, close to the helm and ready for immediate use. Never tie it to its holder: if you are worried about security, bring it inboard whenever you leave the boat.

Gas Detectors

Gas and petrol vapour, being heavier than air, can collect in the bilges of the boat. If there is a persistent leak somewhere, this can build up over the months and present a real risk of explosion. A gas detector will warn you with an audible alarm before the build-up becomes a problem. Some models will also shut off the gas supply automatically.

You can also buy bilge water-level detectors that warn you of rising water in the bottom of the boat. These are more or less superfluous if you have an automatic bilge pump (which is dealt with below). Do not be misled by advertisers' claims that their detector can monitor both water and gas; they may detect water, but if they do they will never 'smell' gas again as the sensor will have been wrecked.

Gas has to be treated carefully – a leak could endanger everyone aboard. Cylinders should be stowed outside the accommodation and turned off when not in use.

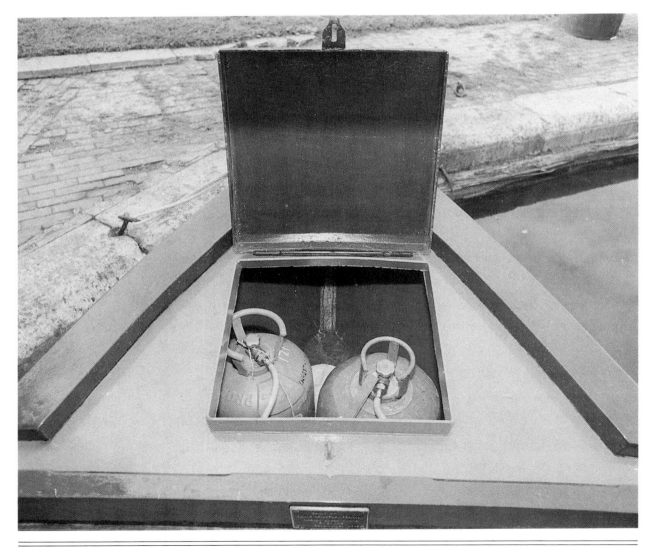

Bilge Pump

Keeping the water on the outside of the boat where it belongs is a priority. Any boat that has a raised sole, and therefore cannot be emptied with a bucket or bailer – which means effectively any boat with accommodation – should carry at least one manual bilge pump. This can be supplemented with an electric pump, either switch-operated or automatic, but you should never have to rely on there being electricity to be able to pump out.

The manual pump should be fixed in position somewhere on deck, where it can be operated without having to go below. Most boats will have a single bilge, with what are called limber holes cut in the frames to allow water to drain through from section to section, so the intake should be sited at the lowest point. It is well worth fitting a longer suction pipe than necessary so that if the limber holes are blocked up, the intake can be moved instantly to another part of the bilge.

Horn

All boats should have an audible means of attracting attention, to warn of their approach or to call for help in an emergency. They can also be used to make special signals to other craft. An electric or aerosol horn is best, the squeeze-bulb type not having enough power.

Torch

A powerful torch is a must, whether or not you intend to do any night cruising. The best type is a rechargeable handlamp which has a combined bracket and 12V charger. Although relatively expensive – typically about £30 – it saves you having to buy batteries, which for a big torch are seldom cheap.

First-aid Kit

The aim of first aid is not necessarily to treat injuries, but to prevent them from getting worse before the casualty can receive proper medical attention. On some of the more remote waterways you can travel for an hour or more between waterside dwellings, so if there is a medical emergency on board you may have to keep going for quite a while before you reach a telephone. While it is impractical to cater for every eventuality, a rudimentary knowledge of how to deal with the more common injuries and a modest first-aid kit are essential. There are several proprietary kits on the market, but you can easily make up your own with dressings and treatments sold in the local chemists (see the panel overleaf) and this may prove cheaper as well as giving you a wider choice.

BE PREPARED

To give a list of the most likely accidents on board might suggest they are more common than they are, or that boating is more dangerous than it is. Happily, the chances are that your cruising will never be marred by any medical emergency more serious than an insect sting, a case of sunburn or a bad hangover.

While on the subject of hangovers, most of the ailments that might lay a crew low are self-inflicted, the result of incautious over-indulgence in food, drink or both. But in a warm boat with a faulty fridge food can go off surprisingly quickly, and water left in the tanks can also go bad. Keep a check on these, and do not dismiss an upset tummy, especially if more than one person is suffering.

Unlikely though they might be, accidents happen in the best-regulated boats, and if you are heading into the countryside, away from phone boxes and casualty wards, it pays to be prepared. You should know how to deal with severe cuts, burns, scalds, minor fractures, shock, unconsciousness and drowning, all of which are covered in first-aid courses run by the St John Ambulance, St Andrew's Ambulance Association and the Red Cross. If you do not have the time or the inclination to take a course, the *First Aid Manual* published jointly by the three organizations is excellent value at £3.95. The book and details of courses are available from headquarters offices (see the Appendix) and from branch offices, whose addresses will be found in local telephone directories.

First-aid kits should be packed in a dry, waterproof box. A very basic kit might contain:

> For headaches and other pains: paracetamol
> For tummies: kaolin and morphine (anti-diarrhoea), milk of magnesia (antacid)
> For sunburn: calamine lotion
> For bites and stings: Wasp-Eze
> For burns, scalds, and as a general antiseptic: Germolene

Injuries other than burns should be dressed. A pack of plasters will do for most purposes, but more serious injuries will require proper dressings. The *First Aid Manual* suggests:

> 10 individually wrapped adhesive plasters
> 1 sterile eye pad
> 1 triangular bandage
> 1 sterile covering for a serious wound
> 6 safety pins
> 3 medium-sized sterile unmedicated dressings
> 1 large sterile unmedicated dressing
> 1 extra large sterile unmedicated dressing
> Several 1-ounce packs of cotton wool
> Tweezers
> Scissors

WILDLIFE OF THE WATERWAYS
by Frances Moon

It is an unforgettable experience for town dwellers to wake at their inland mooring and hear nothing but the sound of birdsong, or to wander away from the boat on an early autumn morning and find a spider's web bejewelled with dewdrops. Living close to nature is the dream of many people in this mechanized age, but for most it is only on holiday that it can be realized. Cruising on the inland waterways brings you exceptionally close to a great variety of wild living things. Birds and animals that would flee from a walker are not afraid of moving boats.

Canal banks have been made green by nature and act as unofficial wildlife reserves. Foxes live beside canals in towns, and many plants have spread along railways and towpaths. An example is the Oxford ragwort: originally from Sicily, growing in volcanic ash, it was carefully nurtured in the Botanic Garden at Oxford, but escaped and soon colonized most of the country. Its bright yellow flower heads provide cheerful colour beside urban waterways and offer a home to caterpillars of the cinnabar moth.

On inland waterways you can watch birds like heron, kingfisher, moorhen, mallard and mute swan and glimpse brightly coloured dragonflies. On canals in particular are a great variety of plant and habitat types, changing all the time as you travel along. Stretches of open water will be succeeded by grassy banks rich with wild flowers. Woods, scrubland, moors, wetland and marshes: each supports a different community of plants, animals, birds and insects.

The water channel itself is important for swans and other water birds, aquatic insects and plants that float or grow mostly submerged. At the water fringe grow marsh plants that like to have their roots in water, and here too may be found frogs, toads and grass snakes. Young dragonflies make their home here. A towpath of mown and trampled grass supports a variety of meadow flowers and butterflies. The hedgerow provides essential shelter for many birds and insects: it may include edible berries that keep the feathered population alive through the winter. On the opposite side of the waterway may be woodland and scrub, home for another colony of wild creatures. If the trees include some dead timber, woodpecker, nuthatch and owl may be present, with insects like wood-boring beetles.

The descriptions of plants and animals that follow provide a general guide to some of the more common species you can expect to see, but are far from comprehensive. You will need some reliable reference books with clear colour pictures to establish an identification beyond reasonable doubt. The paperback version of *The New Concise British Flora* by W. Keble Martin is light enough to carry with you (please take the book to the plant, not the plant to the book). *The Shell Guide to the Birds of Britain and Ireland* by James Ferguson-Lees, J. R. T. Sharrock and Ian Willis is less portable, being a hardback, but can be kept in the boat's cabin.

ANIMALS AND PLANTS OF THE WATER

Mallard

Everyone knows the common mallard duck, with its adorable yellow chicks in spring. The female is mottled brown and quacks loudly, but the quieter drake has a striking iridescent head colouring of green with blue and purple where it catches the light. There are many other types of duck that can be seen at the Wildfowl Trust Reserve, Slimbridge, near Gloucester, on the River Severn estuary.

Moorhen

The shy moorhen has long, spindly green legs and feet ideal for walking over mud or floating plants. It is smaller than a mallard, with a black body, red beak and distinctive black and white feathers under the tail. It eats plants, seeds, insects, tadpoles and small fish, and nests on a well-constructed platform of water plants in shallow water.

Coot

Coots are predominantly black birds with a large white flash on the beak. Their characteristic sound is a loud honking. Coots dive for weed to eat and can stay underwater for at least half a minute. They are fiercely territorial, and recently each side pond of the Devizes flight of locks on the Kennet & Avon Canal was occupied by a single pair of coots.

Mute Swan

Poets and writers have long extolled the pure white swan, which makes no sound but was supposed to sing beautifully before it died. Swans are immensely strong (a blow from a wing can break a man's arm), so beware when they are nesting. At other times they can be almost embarrassingly friendly, crowding round your boat for scraps of bread,

Coot on nest.

even knocking on the hull with their beaks when they feel a mealtime is due. Swans in flight, usually at dusk, make an extraordinary creaking sound with their wings. The famous 'ugly ducklings', or cygnets, stay with their parents and keep the mottled brown feathers until they are a year old.

Heron

This impressive grey bird can have a wing span of over 6 feet. It looks almost prehistoric in flight, with its head sunk between its shoulders. Herons stand upright and motionless at the water's edge, looking for fish. They will suddenly stab down into the water with a sharp beak. Heron nests are untidy platforms of twigs improbably balanced at the top of large trees. There are a number of heronries close to waterways — for instance, at Gailey reservoir near the Staffordshire & Worcestershire Canal between Wolverhampton and Stafford.

Kingfisher

A flash of iridescent blue is often the only sign of this beautiful bird. It is only about 6½ inches long, has a reddish breast and a long dagger-like beak. It feeds almost entirely on fish by diving into slow-moving water, hovering before plunging in if there is no perch nearby. It may starve if canals are iced over for long periods in winter. Kingfishers live even in the East End of London; for instance, I have seen them by the Regent's Canal at Victoria Park, Hackney.

Grey heron.

Dabchick

Otherwise known as the little grebe, the dabchick has brown feathers with chestnut colour on the sides of the face and throat and white at the base of the beak. Its favourite wintering places are reservoirs and sheltered estuaries. During the breeding season it lurks in the reeds, but you may see one fleetingly on the canal or river.

Black-headed Gull

The 'bovver boys' of inland waters, these gulls have probably never seen the sea. They scavenge on rubbish tips and will follow a ploughing tractor as if it were a fishing boat. In the summer the gull has a black head, which becomes white in winter with a black dot near the eye.

Great Crested Grebe

This is Britain's largest grebe, a showy bird in summer with red-brown and black frills on the side of the head. It swims low in the water with its head held high, then suddenly dives for fish and can stay submerged for long periods. Its strange courtship dance can be witnessed on breeding waters such as the Grand Union Canal reservoirs at Marsworth, near Tring, Herts.

Dabchick.
Great crested grebe.

Canada Goose

A large goose with a long black neck and head, broad white chin-strap, white breast and brown body, its deafening honking can be heard on many inland waters. Like all geese, Canadas tend to fly in V-formation on long flights to conserve energy.

Dipper

This handsome black and white bird inhabits swiftly flowing streams and rivers. It can be seen bobbing over weirs and among gravel. The bird plunges into the water and walks about to find small fish, worms and other creatures on the river bed. It looks as if it is wearing evening dress, with a white 'shirt-front', black back and dark brown head.

Water Lily

Usually a plant of still water, ponds and lake fringes, the pure white water lily has large flowers with yellow stamens and almost circular leaves. There is also a rich golden variety with much smaller flowers and larger leaves.

Dipper.

Water Boatman

This jolly insect looks just like a boat with its legs as oars when it is on the move through the water. Surprisingly for an insect about half an inch long, it eats tadpoles and small fish. It can also fly considerable distances.

Newt

Newts spend most of their time on land, feeding mainly at night and hiding under stones or logs during the day. In about March they return to ponds and deeper slow-moving waters to breed. The young leave the water about August. The largest British species is the great crested newt, which hibernates between September and March.

Fish

The commonest fish to be found in inland waterways are roach, tench, dace, carp, chub, bream, perch and pike. Salmon and trout are found in the fast-moving upper reaches of rivers. Also present in waterways are eels and the eel-like lampreys. Crayfish (freshwater shellfish) are present in some canals, and transparent freshwater prawns are found only in the River Thames and the Norfolk Broads rivers.

ANIMALS AND PLANTS OF THE WATER MARGIN

Reed Warbler and Sedge Warbler

These inconspicuous brown birds, which keep within the reeds and marsh plants, can be recognized by their warbling song. The sedge warbler has a cream-coloured stripe over the eye and a streaked head; reed warblers make remarkable nests of reeds and grass lined with soft feathers, wool and hair, woven round and supported by several reed stems.

Bittern

Once common in the Broads, this large shy bird is now rare. Its 'booming' call reveals its presence in spring. If alarmed, the bittern freezes with its beak pointing upwards among the reeds, making it almost invisible. The plumage is mottled and barred brown and black.

Swallow

The swallow likes to nest near water and swoops over the surface to catch insects. It has an interesting colouring, if you can spot it perching still for a moment. The back is dark metallic blue, the forehead and throat brown-red, the underside creamy-white. Its forked tail is much in evidence as it dives through the air and it has a twittering song. Swallows are curious birds and will 'buzz' you to get a closer look if you come across them in open countryside.

Sedge warbler.

Bittern.

Grey wagtail.

Wagtail

The bobbing movement of this bird gives away its name. There are two common types – the pied wagtail (black and white) and the grey wagtail, elegantly feathered in grey with touches of yellow underneath.

Curlew

A liquid call is often the most noticeable feature of the retiring curlew. Its feathers are speckled brown and it has long, greenish-grey legs. One of the wading birds, it will be found in river valleys and estuaries, although it also inhabits moorlands. The unusual long curved beak is adapted to extracting worms and shellfish from river mud.

Oyster Catcher

A dapper bird of black and white with long pink legs and a red beak, the oyster catcher is adept at forcing mussel shells open, although its ability to eat oysters is in doubt. The bird is found in estuaries, where it likes to wade in shallow water, also on rivers, inland lochs, reservoirs and gravel pits.

Water vole.

Water Vole

The Water Rat of *The Wind in the Willows*, this likeable creature is not in fact a rat, being related to the field voles. Not to be classed as vermin, it is a harmless animal which eats vegetation and lives in a hole in the river bank. You will often see one swimming across the waterway, then plopping into the water to find the secret entrance to a bankside hole. Conveniently, its dark brown fur is waterproof.

Otter

Everyone loves the otter, with its carefree personality and snub-nosed face. Quite rare in this country, it is now a protected species. The lairs, called holts, are constructed under tree roots or large bankside boulders. The cubs are about three months old before they are introduced to the water, but are able to hunt almost immediately for fish. You can see otters at the Otter Trust, Bungay, in Suffolk.

Frog

The common frog has become much less widespread in the last few years. It breeds in slow-flowing streams, ponds and lakes and leaves dense masses of frogspawn (black eggs in transparent jelly) to the mercy of children with jamjars.

Toad

Toads have shorter legs than frogs, so crawl rather than jump, and are often found in gardens where they should be valued for their ability to catch insects. They are more tolerant of dry conditions than frogs, but, like them, hibernate from about October to March.

Slow-worm

I recently saw a slow-worm on the towpath of the Kennet & Avon Canal. This inoffensive creature is like a small, smooth, glistening brown snake or a large earthworm. It prefers warm, damp sites with plenty of ground cover and was coiling away to hide as I watched it.

Grass Snake

Another harmless reptile, the grass snake is greenish in colour and has a yellow collar. It likes to live near water to feed on frogs and can be seen in the Fens beside drainage channels and waterways.

Dragonfly

Iridescent blues and greens are characteristic of the emperor dragonfly, but gold-ringed and plain brown ones can also be seen. They hover over the water, then suddenly dart off at a tangent while catching small insects. Young dragonflies live in water, but when fully grown the larger varieties may travel miles away from their birthplace.

Willow

Willows have been a feature of the river landscape since early times. Their grey-green foliage of slim, pointed leaves gives them an oriental look. Willows are traditionally pollarded (cut in such a way as to produce a shock of small branches suitable for firewood and hurdles) or treated as osiers. This means chopping them back to ground level so that masses of thin, pliable twigs are formed, ideal for basket-making.

Reedmace

The bulrush of many biblical pictures, reedmace has large, red-brown flower spikes like pokers which appear in late summer, remain like sentinels at the water's edge during the winter and burst about March, releasing clouds of silky white seed-carriers.

Coltsfoot

This attractive flower is a sign of spring, appearing in February or March. The yellow heads were once much more common in meadows and on riversides. They bear clusters of very fine petals which turn into white 'clocks', carrying the seeds away on the wind.

Flowering Rush

An elegant plant with a long, smooth stem bearing a bouquet of bright pink flowers. Each has three petals and a central cluster of large stamens. The rush grows in and beside shallow fresh water.

Cow Parsley

Also known by the romantic name of Queen Anne's Lace, this grows in profusion in summer alongside rivers and canals. It is a member of the umbellifer family, producing white flowers like miniature umbrellas. The parsley-like leaves are inedible, though the plant is related to the carrot family.

Marsh Willowherb

A shortish, rather delicate plant, the marsh willowherb likes to keep its feet damp. The small pink flowers are borne on top of dark green stems with pointed leaves growing in pairs.

Butterbur

This plant has a space-age look that is enhanced when a colony has sprung up in a heap of mud freshly dredged from a waterway. The pink petals are carried on a spike with many flower heads and large curved leaves.

Kingcup

The kingcup or marsh marigold likes to grow in wet places and can be seen at inaccessible spots such as the edge of weirs or lock bypasses, for unfortunately it is one that people love to pick. Its showy, bright yellow cup with clusters of gold stamens grows on hairless stalks, set off by large kidney-shaped leaves. It is not related to the garden marigold.

Celandine

A favourite flower of children, the celandine has glossy, pointed petals of true butter yellow and dark green heart-shaped leaves. Its appearance in February or March is a sure prediction of spring.

Purple Loosestrife

A showy flower enhancing watersides in summer. The petals form rosettes with a few small leaves round the stem and the long flower heads grow in bunches that lean out over the water.

ANIMALS AND PLANTS OF THE WATERSIDE, HEDGEROW AND MEADOW

Skylark

Nothing is more characteristic of summer in open spaces than the skylark's twittering song as it soars heavenwards. Skylarks are unremarkable brown birds that nest on the ground in grass cups lined with finer grasses, usually well hidden among crops or tufts of grass.

Stonechat

The call of this bird of moors and rough meadows can easily be mistaken for the clicking of one pebble on another, hence its name. In summer the male has a black head with white patches on either side of the neck and on the wing. The bird constantly flicks its tail and wings while perching on the tops of bushes. In winter it may be found on derelict industrial sites – for instance, near canals.

Yellowhammer

'A little bit of bread and no cheese' describes the monotonous song of this likeable bird, heard in the spring, summer and early autumn. It inhabits open countryside, the edges of woods and industrial sites, where it sits in full view, so that you can easily distinguish the bright lemon-coloured head and underparts of the male.

Goldfinch

Small, colourful birds with red, white and black heads and black-and-yellow wings, goldfinches like to feed on thistle heads. They have specially adapted beaks to pull the seeds from these and other plants with hooks protecting the seeds, such as teasels. Even so, they sometimes become caught on teasel barbs. The birds hang acrobatically while extracting seeds with a rapid 'sushing' sound.

Fox

So much has been written about foxes; suffice it to say that these graceful reddish-brown mammals live in towns as well as the country, inhabit canal banks and railway cuttings and are adept at concealing themselves during the daytime. They eat all kinds of food, including slugs and worms, but are not averse to scavenging fish and chips and scattering the wrappings round city litter bins.

Badger

The distinctive black and white head of the noble-looking badger acts as camouflage in moonlit woodlands. A placid animal, the badger is nevertheless built like a bear and has a powerful gripping jaw. The home (or sett) is built into a slope to avoid flooding and is kept immaculately clean.

Peacock butterfly.

Shrew

This tiny mammal has a long, quivering nose used to investigate its surroundings. Its fur is dark brown on the back and yellowish underneath. There is also a water shrew, Britain's smallest water mammal, which has a black back and silvery fur underneath and spends a great deal of time swimming.

Butterflies

You will see a variety of butterflies near the waterways, depending on the kind of countryside nearby and the food plants it supports. The attractive common blue and brimstone butterflies will be found in grassland, while the marsh fritillary likes damp meadows and rough hillsides. The caterpillars of both the colourful red admiral and the peacock, with its remarkable blue 'eye' markings on the wings, depend on nettles for food and the butterflies will be found near an abundance of these plants.

Hawthorn

When the canals were built, the canal companies were obliged to plant stockproof hedges alongside to prevent farm animals straying. They usually planted hawthorn, and the hedges you see today are the descendants of those original ones of the late eighteenth and early nineteenth centuries. The individual bushes combine to form a thick, thorny hedge which is hard to penetrate, and the craft of laying to maintain the thickness is still practised.

Hawthorn was regarded as a magical plant, bearing the heavily scented may blossom so important to pagan tree-worshippers of the pre-Christian age and still celebrated in maypole and May Queen ceremonies. The white (and rarer pink) blossoms give way to red fruits called haws which provide essential food for hedgerow birds in a hard winter.

Blackthorn

Another hedging plant, less common than hawthorn but still widespread on farmland and beside canals and rivers. The twigs are black, and delicate white flowers appear before the leaves in March. The fruits are purple-black sloes, which can be used to flavour gin.

Ragged Robin

This cheerful-looking flower has ragged-edged pink petals arranged in an untidy coronet. It likes damp meadows and marshy places.

Campion

A relative of ragged robin, the campion has an oval projection at the base of the petals. There are pink and white varieties which like to grow near woods or shady hedges.

Bramble

Canal and riversides in autumn can provide a feast of blackberries, so take something to collect them in! Beware of the prickles, however: the fruit-gatherer can get badly scratched hands. In spring the bramble carries flowers of a subtle mauve-white.

Old Man's Beard

Related to the garden clematis, this decorative plant festoons canal cuttings like the one near Tring, Herts. Also known as travellers' joy, the plant bears small green flowers that turn into pods and release myriads of white seed-carrying parachutes to distribute new plants by wind power.

Rosebay and Great Hairy Willowherb

There are many types of willowherb, but these are the most common. Great hairy willowherb grows in sheaves on the water's edge and has individual pink flowers with rounded petals. Rosebay willowherb bears spires of bright pink blossom which enliven canal sides in summer. It is also known as fireweed because it likes to grow on ground that has been burnt. It became much more widespread after the last war, having colonized bomb sites and waste ground with its wind-blown seeds.

Honeysuckle

The heady scent of honeysuckle speaks volumes about summer. At the base of the stamens is a drop of nectar much sought by bees. The glossy red berries are inedible, except by birds.

Nightshade

A family of plants dwelling in woods and hedges. Beware of the deadly nightshade, every part of which is poisonous. It is known as belladonna (beautiful lady) from the dangerous cosmetic practice of using it to make the eyes shine in past centuries. Later it became a valuable drug for dilating the pupils during eye operations.

Cuckoo Pint

A cluster of bright red poisonous berries is borne on this plant, also known as lords-and-ladies, whose flower is an unusual combination of a single curved green 'petal' (its true name is a spathe) and a brown bullrush-like spike.

Teasel

Small flowers of a tender pale mauve adorn the head of this plant, which develops into an oval seed head covered in barbs to deter birds from eating the seeds. The heads were once used for teasing the tangles out of sheep's wool before it was spun into yarn.

Nettle

Dead-nettles (without stings) can be found with either white or pink flowers; there is a yellow variety, known as yellow archangel. The stinging nettle has green flowers in hanging spikes. The irritation of a nettle sting can be eased by rubbing a dock leaf on to the spot. If pesticides permit, nettles and dock nearly always grow side by side.

Ramsons

A smell of garlic in woodland indicates the presence of these decorative plants, each bearing a halo of white star-like flowers. If the flowers or leaves are bruised, they will give off a stronger scent, and the plant was once used as a flavouring for food.

Meadowsweet

Another perfume redolent of summer, bringing memories of blue skies and calm waters. The blossom is a hazy cloud of tiny cream and gold flowers. Its favoured habitats are marshes, fens, wet meadows, woods and canal banks.

10

MADE IN BRITAIN
by Alan Harper

On a visit to Europe in 1753, the young Duke of Bridgewater was inspired. He saw huge canals, complete with locks, tunnels and aqueducts, busy with barges full of freight. There was nothing to compare with them in Britain.

The Duke owned coal mines at Worsley in Lancashire, and since road transport in eighteenth-century England was virtually non-existent, he decided that what he needed was a canal to take his coal into Manchester. When the Bridgewater Canal opened in 1761, it was hailed as a masterpiece − 'a standing monument of the public spirit and economy of the Duke of Bridgewater to the end of time'.

The man the Duke and his agent, John Gilbert, engaged to build it was James Brindley, a semi-literate millwright from Derbyshire, who as an apprentice had shown such genius for engineering that it used to astound − and dismay − his master. But even before he was approached by the Duke, Brindley had been doing survey work for Liverpool Corporation, which was planning a canal to link the Trent with the Mersey. The canal age had begun.

By the time Brindley died in 1772, at the age of fifty-six, he had been involved with dozens of canal and river projects, from Oxford to the Firth of Forth. An ever-expanding network of canals was spreading across the country, and the foundations had been laid for inland navigation between the four great sea ports of London, Liverpool, Bristol and Hull.

But the early canals were − quite literally − breaking new ground. Their engineers proceeded cautiously, and preferred the safety of following the contours around the landscape to spectacular but risky effects like lock staircases. It is true that there were brilliant engineering achievements − Brindley's original Barton Aqueduct and the first of the two Harecastle Tunnels, for example − but these, too, erred on the side of caution.

The heir to Brindley's throne was Thomas Telford, a Scottish stonemason who, as architect and engineer, left his mark on the industrial landscape like no man before or since. In the phenomenal second phase of canal building, he and his contemporaries built on the experience of their forebears and imposed their will on the landscape. Earlier canals were straightened and widened; new ones were bored through mountains and carried high across valleys on magnificent aqueducts. Cast iron, the wonder material, was worked into bold new ideas.

But there is more to the fabric of the canals and rivers than their monumental structures or the patterns they make on a map. Some of the most pleasing aspects of their architecture are the small details in the great scheme of things — the little farm bridges, perfect in their honest design and solid, functional construction; or the old cast-iron winding gear, intricate and sculptural, reflecting the iron-master's pride in his craft.

LOCKS

Locks are what make inland navigation possible. On any river, a boat travelling upstream will reach a point where the flow is too fast or the water is too shallow for it to go any further.

The first locks were no more than weirs built to dam the stream, thus deepening the water above them and slowing down the flow. To allow boats through, they had movable sections. Later developments of these, called flash locks or staunches, had lifting gates with counterbalances which could be cranked up to let boats underneath. Obviously, when a staunch was opened a huge length of river would have to drain out before the upper and lower water levels met. The boatman going down could attempt to save time by riding the flood through the staunch, which was hazardous; the boatman heading upstream could try to haul his craft through, against the flow. Either way, these primitive locks were far from efficient — although some survived on the fens and the Upper Thames into the early part of this century.

The pound lock — basically two flash locks close together — first appeared in Britain on the short Exeter Canal in 1566, and then on the Thames from the early 1600s. The original locks on the canal had vertically lifting gates at each end, like staunches; those on the river had swinging gates. Both types are still seen today, although swinging gates are more common.

On a canal, where water supply might be a problem, the great disadvantage of locks is the fact that they use water. Every time a boat locks through, a chamberful — many thousand of gallons — flows down into the lower pound.

This difficulty was uppermost in James Brindley's mind when he planned the Trent & Mersey Canal. The crucial dimension of this waterway was the 7-foot width dictated by the Harecastle Tunnel, and he kept its locks down to this size so that they would use as little water as possible. This and the length he decided upon – around 72 feet – determined the size of the standard working narrowboat.

While this standard size is found on almost all the narrow canals, locks on the rivers and broad canals come in various shapes and sizes. The earliest had turf sides, with wooden piles to keep the boats off. Since then lock chambers have been built of brick, stone, concrete or even – as at Beeston on the Shropshire Union Canal – of iron. And although most lock chambers are basically rectangular in shape, there are diamond-shaped locks on the Oxford Canal and the Warwickshire Avon, and restoration work on the Kennet & Avon Canal has included rebuilding the unusual stone arcs in the lock walls at Aldermaston.

It might be true that the principle behind all pound locks is the same, but there is great variety in the methods and equipment used to fill and empty them. At Worsfold on the Wey Navigation the wooden paddles in the lock gates are raised and lowered by hand, and held in place with pegs. But as the canal age got under way, iron rack-and-pinion systems with windlass-operated spindles became increasingly common. Mounted on the balance beams, some of the earlier examples of these have a positively sculptural quality, with all their moving parts in view – as though the engineers and iron-masters were proud of their ingenuity.

Diamond-shaped lock chambers on the Lower Avon.

Particularly interesting paddle gear of this type can be seen on the Shropshire Union and Oxford Canals. In some cases parts or all of the winding gear were encased in iron to protect them from the elements, which is more practical but less attractive. The same applies with ground paddle gear mounted on lock sides – some have exposed mechanisms, like those on the Birmingham Canal Navigations or Staffordshire & Worcestershire; others, usually later in date, are enclosed, as on the Welsh canals and some locks on the Grand Union.

Guillotine gates, while needing no paddle gear, nevertheless presented the engineers with problems of their own. Some, such as those on the Nene and Great Ouse, have the gates and counterweights moving up and down in the same rectangular frame. But the lock gate at King's Norton on the Stratford Canal is an example of a much earlier solution – the weight is suspended on one side, and the gate is opened by an ingenious mechanism of wheels, chains and pulleys.

When a lock was built on a river, a weir had to be constructed to carry the main flow around the side of it. But on some canals, too, weirs and channels are also necessary to cope with excess water. There are some fast-flowing weirs alongside locks on the Llangollen and Leeds & Liverpool Canals, while on the Grand Union the excess water is carried in an open channel. The most celebrated weirs are those on the

Guillotine lock gates on the Great Ouse.

Lock and lockbridge on the Trent & Mersey Canal.

Staffordshire & Worcestershire Canal. Circular, built in brick and covered by rounded iron cages, they lead the water underground to the pound below the lock.

Most locks have footbridges, to make locking easier. Some are simply walkways with handrails, running across the lock gates, but others are more ornate, and there are many individual styles. They were always built at the lower ends of locks, to save making them unnecessarily high. Usually they are models of economy, like the plain wood and iron cantilevers on the Trent & Mersey Canal – some with slots to allow the towrope to pass through – or the basic painted wooden structures at many locks on the Leeds & Liverpool and Grand Union. However, others were more substantial. There are attractive cast iron footbridges on the Macclesfield and Staffordshire & Worcestershire Canals, and heavy brick constructions on the Leicester section of the Grand Union which are part of the structure of the lock.

Of course, horses also had to pass by locks, and could not be expected to negotiate narrow steps and footbridges. Where the towpath was obstructed, a roving bridge might be built to carry it over to the other side, or, as at the sixteen locks at Marple on the Peak Forest Canal, a horse-tunnel could take them round to the other side.

One detail of lock construction which is easily missed is the vertical groove often found in the chamber walls by the upper gates. These are for stop planks, which are slid down to dam the lock for maintenance work. Some locks have a supply of these planks stored by the side, ready for use.

Hard work: Bingley Five-Rise, a staircase of five locks on the Leeds & Liverpool Canal. Once you are at the top you have a 16-mile rest till the next lock.

Part of the charm of older locks is the way in which time and constant use have matured their fabric, until they seem almost an organic part of the landscape. The shapes adopted by the engineers to solve the problems of each individual lock are often both functional and graceful. Worn stone steps and weathered brickwork have a way of looking as though they have always been there. Mooring bollards of iron and wood are sculpted by ropes into strange forms, and iron curbs and rollers fitted to protect the masonry bear the deep scars of years ago, when every boat was pulled through by horse.

When particularly steep slopes were encountered by the engineers, staircase locks – with no pounds between them – were often the answer. Some of these are quite spectacular. The five-lock staircase at Bingley on the Leeds & Liverpool, which raises the canal 60 feet, was hailed when it was built as one of the wonders of the waterways. There are many other staircases on the canals, the main ones being at Banavie, Muirtown and Fort Augustus on Telford's massive Caledonian Canal, and at Foxton and Watford on the Leicester arm of the Grand Union.

But staircase locks use a great deal of water, because the lower chamber always has to be empty before the upper one can be drained.

To get around this problem, some locks incorporate side ponds — reservoirs into which the locks empty — so that the water is not wasted when it is drained out; it can be used later to fill the lower chamber. One of the earliest examples of this principle was built by Brindley at Bratch on the Staffordshire & Worcestershire, consisting of separate locks built at right-angles to the staircase — in effect working as artificial pounds.

Of course, locks are not the only way to take a boat up the side of a hill. The first boat lift on the British canals — on the Ketley Canal, which was built to carry coal and ironstone to Ketley ironworks — dates from 1789. Since this waterway carried rather one-way traffic, the weight of the loaded boats moving down the slope was used to pull the empty boats up. They were carried dry, in cradles. Other 'inclined plane' systems involved hauling huge tanks of water — actual sections of the canal, complete with boats — up slopes. The biggest of these was opened in 1900 at Foxton, where two huge lock-sized tanks were hauled sideways on rails, one counterbalancing the other. The difference in water level was 75 feet. But it proved uneconomic, and little of it now remains.

The Anderton Lift, built in 1875, is the only relic of this era of engineering experiment which is still in use — although repair work following a breakdown in 1983 may only restore it to half working capacity. This great edifice has two 250-ton tanks each capable of carrying two narrowboats up the 50 feet between the River Weaver and the Trent & Mersey Canal.

The Anderton Boat Lift, near Northwich — no longer in operation, but it is hoped to get one of the two chambers working again.

BUILDINGS

With any civil engineering project, money is usually what makes the decisions. Canal companies working on new schemes would often employ an eminent engineer as a consultant, but most of the major building work, from tunnels and aqueducts to company offices, was usually done by their own resident engineer. Lesser structures like workshops, lock cottages and warehouses were often built by local contractors.

The great attraction of most canal building, particularly from the early period, is its simplicity. The contractors usually followed the local styles, and used the locally available materials. In the Midlands, for example, brick was used for most building work, and brickworks were often set up nearby, using clay from the canal diggings. Further north many of the canals were cut through stone, and so much of the fabric of the canals is built from it. For those doing the building there was no time, money or need to make their work anything but functional.

Perhaps the most obvious examples of this design philosophy are the lock cottages. Although they come in many different styles and types, they seldom display any conscious ornament. Those on Telford's Shropshire Union Canal tend to have wide overhanging eaves, and bay windows to allow the keeper to watch for approaching boats. Taller cottages often have single observation windows on their upper storeys, looking down the length of the canal. Some cottages are quite eccentric in design, like the two-storey circular towers on the old Thames & Severn, and the low barrel-roofed houses on the southern Stratford Canal. On some later canals an architectural unity was imposed on the buildings. The little bridge-keeper's cottages on the Gloucester & Sharpness Canal, for example, are all classically styled, with Doric columns and porticos.

Few toll-houses survive today. Usually built at canal junctions, they became redundant with the nationalization of the canals and many were demolished. On the Birmingham Canal Navigations they were attractive, small and octagonal. They were also numerous, but only one now remains – at the Black Country Museum, Tipton. A more substantial octagonal toll-house survives at Bratch, on the Staffordshire & Worcestershire Canal.

At many locks the keepers had small day-huts by the lockside for shelter. These were often very crude and basic, but among the more interesting types which survive are the round, windowless brick huts on the Trent & Mersey, and Telford's on the Shropshire Union Canal – also round and brick, but with more sophisticated styling.

Pumping stations, usually placed on each side of a canal summit pound to keep it topped up, were often built in a plain style which belied their importance. But the huge engines concealed inside, as at Crofton and Claverton on the Kennet & Avon Canal, are anything but mundane. The pump house at Tringford, on the Wendover branch of

*The Clock Warehouse,
Shardlow, on the Trent &
Mersey Canal, now restored
as a canal museum.*

the Grand Union, has big arched windows and affects a more elegant appearance.

The many warehouses, basins and wharves on the canals are reminders of the waterways' commercial origins. And some manufacturing industries soon discovered the benefits of a canalside site. The great potter Josiah Wedgwood was one of the original sponsors of the Trent & Mersey, and he built his famous Etruria factory on the canal near Stoke-on-Trent. Unfortunately this has not survived, but the fine flint and bone mill which used to serve it can still be seen nearby, at the junction with the Caldon Canal. The new Wedgwood pottery of 1940 was also built on the canal, at Barlaston, a few miles to the south; and 11 miles along the Caldon from the Trent & Mersey Canal is the picturesque Cheddleton flint mill, surrounded by workers' cottages, its grinding machinery driven by two waterwheels.

The largest and best-known warehouses were usually built in the centres of cities. Following years of dereliction, some of these have been restored – Gloucester Docks are particularly fine, and so is the recently refurbished Albert Dock in Liverpool – but many have been lost. At Ellesmere Port, Telford built three gigantic 'wing' warehouses on arches over the canal basin, which allowed boats to pass underneath for loading. They were recently demolished after being gutted by fire. But the nearby Boat Museum still makes the port worth a visit.

Canal company headquarters and maintenance yards make interesting groups of buildings, and many of them have survived intact. Some are still being used for their original purpose by the British Waterways Board. The yard at Northwich on the River Weaver is well preserved, and so are Red Bull Yard near the junction of the Macclesfield and the Trent & Mersey Canals, and the old Coventry Canal Co. headquarters at Hartshill with its red brick walls, slate roofs and elegant dock building.

As well as office buildings, these yards needed stables, boat sheds and dry docks, workers' cottages and workshops. Many of them also had ornate clock towers – not simply to add style or prestige to the company premises, but to remind people when they should be working.

Stable buildings were also built at lock flights and tunnels – natural halts where horses could be fed and watered. These halts could also attract pubs and inns. Canal junctions were another natural magnet for settlement.

For the earliest canals, following the contours of the land often meant that they could not pass very close to the towns along the way. When this happened the town's wharves and all its other canal buildings would end up some way outside the town itself. Hanbury Wharf, for instance, on the Worcester & Birmingham Canal, is a fair distance from Hanbury.

Stourport, an entire new town built by Brindley on the junction of the Staffordshire & Worcestershire Canal and the River Severn, still contains all the elements of the first great phase of canal construction. It has four locked basins, warehouses, a BWB maintenance yard, an Italianate clock tower and a large canal company hotel. There is even a surviving row of small workers' cottages – now listed buildings.

BRIDGES

As the first sparks of the industrial revolution flickered to life in the middle of the eighteenth century, two pioneering bridges were built which pointed the way forward for the engineers of the future.

At Pontypridd in 1755 a young prodigy of a mason called William Edwards built a 140-foot single-arch stone bridge over the Taff, which was hailed as the largest span achieved since Roman times. A feature of its design was the three cylindrical holes in each shoulder of the arch, which lightened the structural load without detracting from its strength. And over the Severn at Coalbrookdale, John Wilkinson's famous iron bridge was completed in 1779 – the boldest use yet discovered for the material.

Telford's and Outram's massive aqueducts of iron and stone hark back to the lessons of these two monumental structures, with the complex latticework of Telford's magnificent Galton Bridge in Birmingham illustrating the progress made in fifty years of cast-iron construction. But initially the scale of work on the canal was very much smaller.

OPPOSITE AND FOLLOWING PAGES: ILLUSTRATIONS *(i)* TO *(viii)*. *Just a few of the bridges, some dating back to the Golden Age, that span the waterways.*

ABOVE *(i) 'Fancy Bridge', otherwise known as Avenue Bridge, Chillington.*

BELOW *(ii) 'Cherry eye' bridge on the Caldon Canal.*

(iii) Bratch Locks bridge.

The most common type of bridge on the canals was the accommodation bridge. Farmers, their fields bisected by the intruding waterway, needed to get themselves and their animals from one side of the canal to the other. Since no great weights or distances were involved, the bridges were kept very small and basic. Local materials were used to keep down costs and local masons were employed. In the design of these bridges, form followed function. The results are often beautifully simple, the local brick or stone giving the accommodation bridges of each waterway their own particular flavour.

In places where accommodation traffic was light, the engineers often opted for a cheaper, movable bridge down at the water level. Many of these would spend most of their time open, to let the canal traffic through. On the Welsh canals and the Trent & Mersey there can still be seen the 'Dutch' type of lifting drawbridge, which hinges upwards suspended beneath two weighted beams. The lifting bridges on the Oxford Canal have lower, angled balance arms. On the Stratford Canal there are drawbridges operated with the boat's windlass handle.

But on the broad canals lifting was impractical, so swing bridges were built instead. These were used on nearly all the broad canals, but are most often seen today on the Leeds & Liverpool, Grand Union, and in the narrow system on the Peak Forest and Macclesfield Canals.

One broad canal which does have a lifting bridge is the Basingstoke, which is expected to re-open after restoration in 1988. At North Warnborough a hand-cranked hydraulic lifting bridge was built in 1953 to replace a derelict swing bridge. It spans 17 feet and takes forty-five minutes to wind fully open.

In places where engineering difficulties or farmers' land rights forced the towpath over to the other side of the canal, there would either be a horse-ferry – as there used to be on the Upper Thames and the Trent – or a roving bridge, also known as a turnover or changeline bridge. The simplest type of roving bridge was nothing more than a footbridge big enough for a horse, and there are many fine examples of these. But they had a disadvantage – the towrope would have to be untied while the horse went across.

(iv) The extraordinary Drayton Manor footbridge.

(v) Hydraulically-operated lifting bridge on the Caldon Canal.

(vi) Roving bridge, Macclesfield Canal.

(vii) Great Haywood junction bridge.

One way of solving this problem was to build a bridge of two projecting cantilevers, which would not quite meet in the middle – thus leaving a gap for the rope to pass through. Similar bridges were also built at locks. Usually made from cast iron, some also had wooden handrails, and they can be found on the Stratford-upon-Avon and Trent & Mersey Canals. In many of them the gap has closed over the years. On the Birmingham and Worcester Canal, the same principle was applied to single-cantilever bridges, reaching right across the canal with a small gap at one side.

But the most elegant roving bridges are those which led the horse under the arch – so that the rope could stay tied – then over the canal, and down to the boat on the other side. The best-known of this type are those on the Macclesfield and Peak Forest Canals. With their spiralled pathways, attractive stonework and functional simplicity they are among the most graceful constructions on the waterways. There is a fine example of one at Marple, at the junction of the two canals.

The best bridges on the waterways derive their beauty from simple, functional design. But there were cases when special efforts were made to create an attractive architectural work – usually when the canal passed through the estate of a wealthy landowner, and at his request. These were often built of stone in the classical style, with cornices and balustrades, in harmony with eighteenth-century English country-house design. There are examples of these at Teddesley Park on the Staffordshire & Worcestershire Canal, and near Wheaton Aston on the Shropshire Union.

(viii) Cast-iron bridge at Hawkesbury Junction.

The Macclesfield Bridge on the Regent's Canal at Regent's Park in London is also highly ornamental. Built of brick and iron in 1829, this bridge was blown up in an accident in 1874 by a barge carrying gunpowder. It was rebuilt using its original fluted Doric columns, but these were put back the wrong way round – the rope-grooves worn in the iron now face away from the canal.

AQUEDUCTS

When James Brindley planned his first aqueduct, to take the Bridgewater Canal over the River Irwell, people laughed. It was described as 'a castle in the air'. When he built it, however, laughter turned to amazement and admiration.

There had been aqueducts before in England – the New River, built in 1616 to run a water supply from the Hertfordshire countryside to Islington, used lead-lined timber trunking and brick arches to carry the stream across roads and rivers – but there had been nothing on such a huge scale. Brindley's massive stone structure, reaching 600 feet across the valley, carried the canal nearly 40 feet up on three rounded arches. The centre one was 57 feet across. The aqueduct was 36 feet wide – 18 feet of canal, 6 feet of clay puddle lining, and 12 feet of packed earth and parapet. The local population were reassured by its bulk – it was not going to collapse and flood the countryside – while the engineers were shown that such things were indeed possible.

This first great aqueduct was demolished in the 1890s with the building of the Manchester Ship Canal. It had a worthy successor – the huge Barton Swing Aqueduct, 235 feet long and 1,400 tons in weight. But Brindley built many more aqueducts. The Staffordshire & Worcestershire Canal is carried over the River Sow at Milford on a series of low brick arches, and the twenty-three-arch structure at Stretton is his most famous, carrying the Trent & Mersey Canal for over a mile in its crossing of the River Dove.

None of his subsequent aqueducts was ever as high as his first. Indeed, the very solidity of his heavy stone and brick construction prevented any great heights being achieved. The huge tiered Roman aqueducts, towering over 100 feet high at Segovia and Nîmes, were built as part of a water supply system, not to carry the great weight of a canal. They could therefore have that delicacy of construction which makes their layered rows of stone arches appear almost weightless.

BELOW AND FOLLOWING PAGES: ILLUSTRATIONS *(i)* TO *(v)*. *Without doubt the most dramatic features of the networks are the aqueducts.*

BELOW *(i) Pontcysyllte, on the Llangollen Canal.*

However, the finest stone aqueduct on the British waterways is a match for the achievements of the Roman engineers. Completed in 1800 at Marple on the Lower Peak Forest Canal, its three massive arches stride across the Goyt valley almost 100 feet above the river. It was designed by Benjamin Outram, who followed the example of William Edwards' bridge at Pontypridd and built hollow cylinders into the shoulders of the arches to save weight. These, together with the contrasting colours of stone and brick along the parapet, divide up what would otherwise be oppressive areas of masonry and lend the giant structure a feeling of lightness and elegance.

Yet, to build in stone on such a scale was not always practical. Outram's Marple Aqueduct almost bankrupted the canal company, and delayed the completion of the sixteen Marple locks for five years. In future such ambitious projects would have to rely on iron.

In fact the first iron aqueducts had already been built. Outram's first on the Derby Canal and Telford's much larger edifice near Longdon-on-Tern on the Shrewsbury Canal had both opened within a month of each other in 1795. But these could not compare with Telford's monumental answers to the challenges of the Llangollen Canal.

(ii) Hazlehurst Aqueduct, the 'Caldon Canal flyover'.

Presented with the deep valleys of the Rivers Dee and Ceiriog, he realized that the canal could either run through a tortuous series of locks to take it low enough for stone aqueducts, or it could be carried on its existing level, high above the valley floors, in troughs of iron.

The first of these aqueducts to be completed was Chirk, in 1801. This appears to be built in stone, but its tall arches and slender parapet were only made possible by the iron trough bearing the canal, 70 feet above the valley floor. It has been suggested that Telford felt obliged to disguise Chirk's iron core with stone, after the lukewarm reception of his rather stark and basic aqueduct at Longdon – thus dressing radical ideas in familiar clothes to make them more acceptable.

But he felt no such inhibitions at Pontcysyllte. The slim iron channel, balanced 120 feet up on delicately tapered stone pillars and running arrow-straight for 1,000 feet across the valley, is the most famous sight on the British waterways, and one of Telford's greatest achievements. The aqueduct is a monument to the industrial age, and a powerful expression of the supremacy of iron. It was opened in 1805, after ten years of construction.

Telford's iron-trough principle is often seen on a smaller scale. These

(iii) Chirk Aqueduct, also on the Llangollen.

(iv) Barton Swing Aqueduct.

aqueducts are usually simple box-like structures carrying the waterway over a road or railway in a single, straight span, their harsh square shapes, with no need of an arch, emphasising the brute strength of the material. One of them carries the Grand Union Canal over the Ouse at Wolverton, near Milton Keynes. Built in about 1808 to replace a three-arched stone structure which collapsed, the trough runs across the cutting, supported by a single pillar.

As Telford grew more confident about the use of iron, his work began to combine structural detail with more ornate design. The Stretton Aqueduct, bearing the Shropshire Union over the A5 – one of Telford's own roads – is a good example. Built in 1832, it proudly displays the secrets of its construction, with solid stone piers, exposed nuts and rivets and decorative iron railings coming together in industrial-age harmony. This decorative style reached its finest expression in the Birmingham Canal Navigations. Telford's Engine Arm aqueduct over the New Main Line is a masterpiece, its rows of fine Gothic arches anticipating Victorian ecclesiastical ornamentation.

But although iron had demonstrated its potential over the Welsh valleys, aqueducts of stone and brick continued to be built – with poor road transport, canal engineers were dependent on locally available materials. The Macclesfield Canal, completed some twenty-five years after the Pontcysyllte Aqueduct, is taken over the Trent & Mersey Canal and several roads and railways on elegant brick and masonry structures.

John Rennie's two famous aqueducts, over the River Lune on the Lancaster Canal, and the Dundas Aqueduct on the Kennet & Avon Canal, are both classically styled and built in stone, their cornices and balustrades lending a Renaissance delicacy to their considerable size. The Lune Aqueduct, built in 1797, is particularly massive – its five 75-foot arches carry the canal more than 60 feet above the river. The 150-foot-long Dundas Aqueduct, near Limpley Stoke, dates from 1805. It has been restored along with much of the rest of the Kennet & Avon Canal, which is expected to re-open in 1988.

Sometimes the natural order of events was reversed, when aqueducts were added to canals long after their completion. When a railway in the process of construction had to pass underneath a canal, the delicate engineering problem arose of having to build an aqueduct with the canal already in place. Often this considerable feat was achieved without disturbing the canal. At Frimley on the Basingstoke Canal a two-arched aqueduct was built, not without difficulty, by the London & South Western Railway Co. in the 1830s. In 1900, as the railway expanded to four tracks, two more arches were added.

(v) Lune Aqueduct, Lancaster Canal.

TUNNELS

The vast differences in the two phases of canal building in Britain are illustrated by the pair of 1½-mile Harecastle Tunnels, between the Bridgewater and the Trent & Mersey Canals.

The first one, begun in 1766, took eleven years to complete. Brindley determined its width – and the widths of the Trent & Mersey Canal and the standard narrowboat – from the boats used in the Duke of Bridgewater's colliery tunnels at Worsley. There was no towpath.

Sixty years on, the second Harecastle Tunnel, complete with towpath, was built by Telford in less than three years. Such was the progress made in engineering expertise.

The canal engineer, faced with a hill, had several choices. He could go round it; he could build locks to carry the canal over it; he could make a cut through the hill, if it were not too high; or he could bore a tunnel through to the other side. The first two options were very time-consuming for boats; locks were also expensive to build and used a lot of water. But cuttings were difficult to maintain, and prone to landslips, which could block the canal. Often a tunnel was the only viable proposition.

In some cases the need for a water supply for the canal was the main reason for digging a tunnel. The one at Greywell on the Basingstoke Canal – now collapsed – was dug not only as a short cut, but to tap underground springs in the chalk.

Long tunnels were not simply dug through from one end to the other. In order to have as many teams of men working as possible, holes were sunk into the hill down to the level of the canal, and the tunnel was dug in line until the teams joined up. This called for great accuracy from the surveyors, but most canal tunnels are remarkably straight. In some it is possible to see where the teams met up – the walls have slight kinks in them every few hundred yards.

The original vertical shafts were usually lined with brick when the tunnel was finished, and used for ventilation. Following the line of a tunnel over a hill it is sometimes possible to see traces of excavated earth alongside the shaft chimneys. Where there appear to be more of these mounds than actual shafts, the workings were probably filled in rather than lined in order to cut costs.

There is often evidence in the contrasting portals at each end of a tunnel that they were built by different teams of workmen. The two ends of Preston Brook Tunnel on the Trent & Mersey Canal are completely different in character – the mouth of the southern portal tapering slightly towards the top and faced with stone, the northern portal flatter in shape and built in plain brick. The portals of the Greywell Tunnel shared the same design details – including the circles inscribed in the shoulders of the arches, reminiscent of William Edwards' bridge at Pontypridd – but the features' positioning was completely different.

Some tunnels have towpaths, but unless they are short enough to be relatively light inside, like the Cowley Tunnel on the Shropshire Union, it is best if passengers return to the boat for the transit.

The three parts of the 3154-yard Dudley Tunnel make it the longest still-navigable tunnel in the canal system.

Some shorter, shallower tunnels were dug first as cuttings, and then covered over. Once the engineers had mastered the art of stabilizing cuttings to prevent landslips, some of these tunnels were opened out again. This was done at the summit level of the Oxford Canal, on a length still known as The Tunnel. The short Armitage Tunnel on the Trent & Mersey Canal was opened out in 1971 after nearby colliery workings caused subsidence in the roof.

The longest tunnel built on the British canal cystem was the 3-mile Standedge Tunnel on the Huddersfield Narrow Canal. This crosses the Pennines more than 600 feet above sea level, and some of its working shafts had to be sunk 600 feet down from the hillside to the canal level. The canal closed in 1944. The longest tunnel still navigable is at Blisworth on the Grand Union Canal at 3,056 yards long, although the three separate lengths of the Dudley Tunnel in Birmingham are slightly longer. The shortest of the forty-six surviving tunnels – at 25 yards – is at Dunsley on the Staffordshire & Worcestershire Canal.

Some tunnels are supposed to be haunted. A ghost called Kit Crew or Kit Crewbucket apparently lives at the Turnrail, where Telford's Harecastle Tunnel cuts Brindley's colliery branch to Golden Hill. He is also claimed by a number of other tunnels, although his origins are obscure. And at Saddington Tunnel on the Leicester section of the Grand Union there is said to lurk the spectre of a woman without a head. Keep your eyes open, and a clove of garlic in your oilskins.

11

TRAILING

While the walking-speed pace is one of the joys of canal and river cruising, enabling you to make the most of the unmatched peace of the waterways, it does have one great drawback. At 4 miles an hour and an average twenty minutes per lock, you will be lucky on some stretches to get 20 miles in a day, which means that you can spend your entire holiday moving from one cruising ground to another.

One answer is to hire (more on that in Chapter 12). But hiring ties you down, with fixed start days, fixed locations, and so on; if you want to be totally independent, and go boating when and where you want to – in a different part of the country every weekend, if you like – you will have to trail.

A BOAT FOR THE ROAD

When trailing, your choice of boat will be limited by the size of your car. The car's engine power is not as important as weight when it comes to controlling a tow: a 1600cc saloon will be physically capable of towing the largest boat its weight allows.

That having been said, with a low-powered car acceleration is likely to be sluggish and it may be difficult on a gradient to maintain the maximum permitted speed. The more ccs you have under the bonnet the better.

If you intend to do a lot of towing, it may be worth getting a four-wheel-drive car. On a normal car the power of the engine is transmitted to the road by a pair of wheels, each of which has an area in contact with the surface about the size of a large shoe. Double the number of driven wheels and you double the traction, reducing the likelihood of wheelspin on wet roads or slipways.

To keep the weight down, a trailable cruiser will usually have an outboard engine, though low-powered outdrives and inboards can sometimes be fitted. Unless you intend to use the boat on fast-flowing rivers or tidal waters, 10–15hp will give an 18- or 19-footer all the power you need. This should allow a top speed of over the limit applying on most rivers.

As was explained in Chapter 7, it pays to be realistic about one's expectations with smaller craft. Very few trailable cruisers offer anything more than overnight accommodation. Although there might be a portable chemical toilet below the berths in the cabin, cooking facilities will be minimal, washing facilities virtually non-existent.

Longer stays on boats of this sort will require some of the skills and attitudes needed by campers. Local hotels or sports clubs can provide the occasional bath, shower and an opportunity to wash clothes, while meals that are beyond the scope of a single-burner cooker can be supplied by pubs and restaurants.

The parallel with camping can be extended further. Listening to rain beating against the cabin roof of a small boat is no more fun than staying in a tent in the rain, so if it starts to bucket down you are better off going ashore for the duration. But for all that, given good weather, the right attitude and above all a sense of humour, a trailing holiday is a practical and relatively cheap way of seeing a lot of different waterways in a short time.

The trouble with boats is that they have to be designed to look good and cruise efficiently. An 18-foot caravan can sleep six, being a lot higher than a similar-sized boat, rectangular rather than triangular or semi-circular in cross-section, and with no space devoted to engine or cockpit; but made to float, it would be incapable of making headway against a wind, difficult to steer and control and, even at waterways speeds, expensive on fuel.

As an interesting aside, thirty-five years ago there was an amphibious caravan called the Otter, made of ply and powered by a small outboard. Broadcaster Raymond Baxter owned one with which he introduced his family to cruising. It was not hugely successful as a design, partly for the reasons already mentioned and partly because it attracted the wrong sort of interest: Raymond Baxter tells the story of one incident when a couple of passers-by returning from the pub rang the police to announce that some hooligans had tipped a caravan into the canal 'with little kids in it'!

TRAILING AND THE LAW

The laws relating to trailing are strict, and often strictly enforced. In practice, any powered boat with accommodation should be carried on a braked trailer. Vehicles towing loads weighing more than the kerbside weight of the car used to be subject to a lower speed limit, but in 1986 the law changed and you can now tow at up to 60mph as heavy a load as the car will pull.

That having been said, it will make towing easier if you keep the ratio of load to kerbside weight below 1:1 if possible. As an illustration, a Shetland Family Four, 17 feet 7 inches long, weighs slightly over half a

ton. By the time you add a 10–15hp outboard engine, gear such as fuel tanks, and a two-wheel trailer, the gross weight of the tow will be approaching a ton. You can tow this combination behind a relatively small car – a 1600cc Maestro or Astra, or a Peugeot 305 – without exceeding the magic 1:1.

Either the trailer or the boat itself must have a rear lighting board with triangular reflectors, a full set of lights – indicators, rear, fog and stop lamps and reversing lamps – together with a replica number plate. This will involve fitting a lighting socket on the rear of the car with a relay under the dash.

The trailer – or rather trailer plus load – should be no longer than 7 metres (23 feet) nor wider than 2.5 metres (8 feet 1 inch), and may not project more than 400 millimetres (1 foot 4 inches) beyond the width of the towing vehicle. If it exceeds these dimensions, you will have to comply with all sorts of other regulations applying to long or wide vehicles.

You should certainly fit a nearside wing mirror. Not only is this essential for safe reversing; it is also a legal requirement if the tow obscures the view in your rear-view mirror.

Another legal requirement is that the tow should have no sharp edges that could injure pedestrians, so if you drive with the outboard in

Even a boat with very little accommodation, such as this planing coastal cruiser, will dwarf the car towing it. A good rule of thumb is to keep the weight of the tow to less than the weight of the car.

167

position on the transôm you should put some form of stout plastic cover over the whole of the bottom unit (propeller, gearcase and skeg).

It is important to discuss the insurance of a trailer and boat with your broker to make sure that they are both covered whether on the road or at the launch site. The standard car insurance policy covers you only for third party damage caused by the trailer when attached to the car, and perhaps for fire and theft. If you want comprehensive insurance, you will almost certainly have to pay an extra premium. Damage to the boat while being towed should be covered by a transit clause in your boat insurance policy.

THE TRAILER

What trailer you use will depend to a great degree on the weight of the boat and how you intend to use it. Almost all models will have a ball hitch coupling at the front end, and it is important to balance the load – that is, position the boat on the trailer in such a way that the load at the hitch does not exceed about 100–150lb – the exact amount varies from car to car. This is still a heavy weight to lift, so most trailers have a jockey wheel that can be wound down, jack-like, to raise the coupling to the height of the towbar. The coupling can then be dropped over the ball on the towbar by winding the jockey wheel up again and swinging it clear of the road surface.

Trailer braking systems are usually of the hydraulically damped overrun type. When the towing vehicle slows, inertia carries the trailer forward in relation to the car, and a hydraulic damper slides along a cylinder in the coupling. This operates a lever that is connected by rod or cable to the brake pads, and pulls the brakes on. The upper part of the lever also serves as a handbrake, which should always be applied when the trailer is detached from the car. A 'breakaway cable' from the lever to the rear end of the car ensures that, in the unlikely event of the ball hitch failing or coming off, the brakes will be applied automatically. With many trailers the brake system has to be disconnected before backing into a space or down a slipway, but more and more models now have auto-reversing brakes which make this unnecessary.

Another valuable feature is a winch. Depending on the design of the trailer, recovering the boat – that is, pulling it out of the water and into its towing position on the trailer – may require more energy than a tired crew can summon at the end of a day's cruise. A wire winch connected to an eye on the stem of the boat will solve the problem. This will have a ratchet so that the boat does not make a last-minute dash back into the water, breaking the winch winder's wrist in the process. Electric winches, powered by the car battery, make the task even easier.

The simplest form of trailer has a rigid A- or T-frame mounted on the axle or (in the case of a four-wheeled trailer) axles. Along the centre of this frame runs a set of waisted horizontal rollers that support the boat's keel. Side bars, or more rollers mounted on swivel brackets, direct the boat on to the trailer and cradle the outboard edge of the hull bottom. Variations on this basic theme include multi-roller assemblies that swivel in two planes and 'breakback' trailers that hinge in the middle so that the rear part of the frame can be angled more steeply to assist recovery.

Without doubt the more sophisticated a trailer design is, the easier it will be to launch and recover the boat. Expense, of course, increases in proportion, as does the trailer's attractiveness to a thief.

Whether the additional features are worth the extra cost depends to a large extent on how often you are going to use the trailer. If the boat is to be taken to its cruising ground at the start of each season, kept in the water for six months and brought back home at the end of the summer, a basic model will do; if you intend to do a lot of trailing, with a launch and recovery every time you go boating, anything that makes the process easier may be welcome.

Should you go for a two-wheel or four-wheel trailer? Two-wheelers can carry up to about three quarters of a ton and are relatively light; four-wheelers are around 50 per cent heavier, thus reducing the maximum load you can carry with any car. One advantage of the four-wheeler is that the extra pair of wheels makes a puncture or blow-out much less dangerous, but again you have to pay extra for that peace of mind.

Launching slipways are found on every stretch of water. Some – because of gradient or material – are considerably easier to launch from than others, and at some you find a slipmaster with tractor who will launch and recover for you.

Mention of punctures brings us to the question of a spare wheel. Trailer wheels are different sizes from car wheels and few garages have them in stock, so without a spare you may have to leave the boat by the roadside and drive miles to the nearest trailer centre. It is worth carrying a spare wheel, and a special jack as well – the one supplied with your car may not be suitable.

SLIPWAYS

Any trailable cruiser will have to be launched from a hard, or slipway, of concrete, metal track or wood (both the latter are rare nowadays). These are dotted up and down the canals and rivers owned and operated by public authorities, boatyards or clubs. There will usually be a charge for use of the facility, each way or for a single launch and recovery. Charges vary considerably, as does the level of co-operation you can expect from the slipmaster; some will look on with superior amusement, others virtually launch the boat for you. The amount charged, incidentally, is rarely an accurate guide to either the state of the slipway or how much assistance you can expect.

A list of slipways is given at the end of this chapter.

HITCHING UP

The reason the ball hitch coupling has become more or less universal is that it is not only strong but also foolproof. Hitching up takes a matter of seconds.

Check that the trailer handbrake is on, then raise the front end of the trailer by winding down the jockey wheel until the coupling is slightly above the level of the tow ball on the car. Back the car up to the trailer so that the tow ball is directly below the coupling, then wind the jockey wheel up again. As the trailer lowers itself on to the tow ball, lift the handle on the hitch and the coupling should settle firmly on the ball. If it does not, you have not got the ball directly under the coupling. Wind the jockey wheel back down, release the handbrake (unless you are on a hill) and try to manoeuvre the trailer into position. If you are on a hill, you will have to adjust the position of the car.

When the trailer is firmly attached to the car, release the handbrake (making sure the car handbrake is on in its place) and attach the breakaway cable to a strongpoint on the car such as the towbar. Then wind the jockey wheel up so that it is clear of the ground and can be swung up out of the way and locked into its towing position.

Uncoupling is the exact reversal of the above procedure, except that there is no need for precision alignment of car and trailer since they are already attached. Swing the jockey wheel down and wind the handle until the wheel is firmly on the ground; apply handbrake, release breakaway cable; continue winding the jockey wheel down with one hand while you lift up the handle on the hitch.

Hitching up gives you an opportunity to check that you have loaded the trailer and distributed the weight correctly. As mentioned before, the noseweight should be between 100 and 150lb for most vehicles. If you don't know what this load feels like, the simplest way of measuring it is to use a pair of ordinary bathroom scales and a length of strong wood; place the scales beneath the coupling, hold the wood vertically between the two and wind the jockey wheel up until the wood is taking the full load. Then read off the noseweight on the scales. If it is too high, move some of the heavier gear on board from forward to aft; too low, shift gear from aft to forward.

All boats should be firmly secured to the trailer at all times on the road. The best method is to use a pair of retaining straps made of wide webbing that spreads the pressure and will not cut into the deck or rubbing strakes. These have different forms of tensioner, some easier to operate than others. Take the webbing from the main frame of the trailer over the deck — through fairleads if these are available, but otherwise anywhere where the deck line is flat and there are no delicate fittings such as canopy hoops — and back to the frame on the other side. Then tighten, making sure that the tensioner is well clear of the hull. However tight the straps are, they will vibrate in the slipstream as you drive along, and the metal edges of a badly-positioned tensioner will constantly slap against the hull with consequent damage to the paintwork or gelcoat.

Lighting boards should be firmly secured, ideally to the transom of the boat at a height of about 4 feet from the road. Check the operation of all lights, including stop lights, each time you reconnect the cable to the socket.

It may be necessary to adjust the position of the engine. The prop should be well clear of the road, but not raised to its fullest extent as this increases the length of the tow unnecessarily and makes the engine more vulnerable to damage when reversing.

Finally, lock the trailer hitch and take a last look round the boat to make sure all gear is safely stowed and that doors, windows and hatches are closed. You are now ready for the road.

DRIVING WITH THE TOW

A car with a boat in tow is an articulated vehicle 30 feet long or more, a fact that it does no harm to remember constantly. The tow will affect the driving and handling characteristics of the car, will swing into the kerb or out towards the crown on corners, depending on your angle of approach, and may tend to 'snap' at the car on uneven surfaces. But it only takes a little practice, and a lot of caution on your first few outings, to acquire the necessary skills to combat this.

The worst thing that can happen under normal circumstances is that the tow develops a swing, surging off to the left, then a bit more to the right, a bit more to the left and so on. If not caught and controlled, this 'snaking' can increase to the point where the tow takes over and the trailer jack-knifes, with disastrous results.

Snaking usually takes place on down gradients. Accelerating sharply would bring the tow back into line, but is not recommended as increasing the speed heightens the risk of a repeat swing. Panic braking, with the foot pressed firmly to the floor, or pumping the brake will do no good at all. The best remedy is to keep the car going straight, ease your foot from the accelerator and let the engine do the braking for you.

High-sided vehicles overtaking you can also provoke snaking by drawing the tow into their slipstream. If you see a lorry or coach pulling out behind you to overtake, ease off the accelerator and edge over to the left side of your own lane so that you are as far as possible from it as it goes by.

Most problems when towing occur on down gradients. The golden rule is to go down hills in the same gear as you would go up them, and use the braking effect of the engine to prevent an unwanted increase in speed. Long hills can make short work of a car's brakes.

If the tow begins to 'pitch', rocking forwards and backwards so that its nose alternately presses down and pulls up on the rear of the car, the trailer suspension may be weak or faulty. More often, however, this indicates that the weight is badly distributed on the trailer. The best way to overcome the problem is to shift the position of some of the heavier equipment carried on board the boat (see the previous section, ('Hitching Up').

Reversing a trailer is easy as long as you remember that turning the car one way will cause the tow to go in the opposite direction. Thus, if you want the tow to go to the left, you need to apply right-hand lock so that the rear of the car heads off to the right. Figure 11.1 shows the principle.

When overtaking slow lorries on a motorway, you may find they flash their headlights as you pass. Don't worry, there is nothing wrong with the tow: this is merely a common courtesy indicating that the rear of your trailer is now in front of them and you can safely pull back into the slow lane. Incidentally, towing in the outside lane of a motorway is strictly prohibited, and one of the surest ways of attracting unwelcome attention from the police. You could even lose your licence.

Figure 11.1. *Reversing a tow. Start with the car and trailer in line (A), if necessary moving forward a short way to ensure this. Reverse, counteracting any tendency of the tow to swing by applying limited lock in the opposite direction – if the tow sheers off to the left (nearside), turn the wheel to the right, and vice versa.*

When you reach the point at which you want to turn, apply opposite lock to the direction of the turn (B). The trailer will begin to swing round. When the tow is facing in the required direction, centre the wheel, and then use it normally to bring the car into line with the trailer: (C) and (D).

It takes very little movement of the steering wheel to get the trailer turning. Do not overdo it, or you may find the car and the tow at right angles to each other, at which point there is no option but to drive forward and start again.

(A)　　(B)

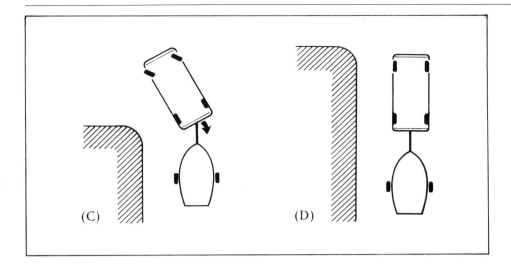

LAUNCHING

Arriving at a crowded slipway on a Saturday, you will be anxious to launch the boat with the minimum of delay. The key is preparation: nothing is more aggravating to others waiting to get afloat than the sight of another boat occupying the slipway for half an hour while its crew mess around with straps and lighting boards. Don't do anything on the slipway that you could have done beforehand.

First, then, park the car and trailer temporarily in the car park while you remove the boat cover, outboard cover and straps. Disconnect the lighting cable from the socket on the rear of the car, and remove the lighting board and cable.

Make sure everything you are going to need is aboard the boat: food, gear and, most importantly, the ignition keys. Secure a long mooring warp to the bow cleat, and leave it coiled on deck ready for use. Raise the engine, using the power tilt if fitted, to its highest position. Check that you have fuel in the tank. Attach the winch wire to the bow eye. You do not have to uncouple the trailer from the car to launch, but just in case you need to do so in a hurry, unlock the trailer hitch if it has been padlocked, and detach the breakaway cable from its anchor point on the car.

Don't hurry the launching. With most trailers the wheels have to be immersed before the boat will float off. If you come straight off the motorway and immediately submerge hot bearings in cold water they will draw in water as they cool. This is less damaging on inland waterways than it is on the coast, where the salt will make short work of the metal, but is nevertheless something to be avoided if possible. Wait for half an hour before launching, to give the bearings a chance to cool.

When you are ready to launch, make the children put on lifejackets or buoyancy aids. Back the trailer down the slipway until the stern of the boat is afloat, lift the ratchet on the winch and give the bow a shove. The boat should now launch itself. If it does not, don't strain yourself: back down a little further and try again.

Once the boat is afloat, get your crew to hold it using the warp you left coiled on deck. You can now uncouple the winch wire and take the car and trailer back up the slipway. The crew may need to go in for some nifty footwork to avoid the trailer frame catching his shins, so take it slowly at first to give him time to get clear.

Park the car and trailer – don't forget to put the trailer handbrake on as well – and you can set off on your cruise.

RECOVERY

This is slightly more complicated than launching because it requires more precision. Switch off the engine and raise the prop, then have your crew hold the boat on the warp while you collect the car and trailer. Back down the slipway to the point where the trailer is an inch or two deeper than was necessary for launching (you don't have gravity on your side this time) – no more, or the boat will not position itself correctly on the trailer. Attach the winch wire to the bow eye, flip the winch ratchet over and, making sure that the boat is straight and the keel is over the centreline rollers, wind the wire on to the drum.

As the boat comes up the trailer and loses the buoyancy provided by the water it will become heavier and therefore more difficult to shift. When it is no longer afloat, check it for position. The keel should be on the centreline, the side bars or rollers supporting parts of the hull bottom equidistant from the keel. If they are not, refloat and try again; don't attempt to push half a ton or more of boat around.

The boat should be winched up until its stem rests against the bow snubber, the roller or pair of rollers mounted high up on the front of the trailer. Give it a final check for alignment, and drive car and trailer back up the slipway. Finally, prepare the tow for the road as outlined in the earlier section entitled 'Hitching Up'.

MAINTENANCE

Upkeep of trailer boats and their engines has already been covered in the relevant chapters. Trailers are simple pieces of engineering, but they do require some maintenance. The hitch should be inspected regularly and greased if it is stiffening up, and the same applies to brake linkages and the hydraulic damper, which should slide easily in its cylinder. Brake cables should be checked and adjusted if necessary, wheel hubs should be kept greased to repel the water, and tyre pressures should be monitored carefully (don't forget to check the pressure of your car tyres, which will need to be increased when you are towing – see your owner's handbook). Finally, the rollers should be free to roll.

TRAILER LAUNCHING SITES

There are well over a hundred slipways throughout Britain's inland waterways network where motor cruisers can be launched free or for a small charge. Not all are attended, and not all are suitable for all sizes of trailable boat. If possible, it is always worth making an exploratory visit beforehand without the boat in tow. The list below is not comprehensive, but includes a good selection of the available sites. It was taken from *Where To Launch Your Boat*, published by Barnacle Marine, which carries more detail than we have space to include here.

Rivers

Avon (Bristol): Saltford Marina, The Shallows, Saltford, Keynsham; Portavon Marina, Bitton Road, Keynsham.

Avon (Warwickshire): Stratford Marina, Clopton Bridge, Stratford-upon-Avon; Evesham Marina, Evesham; Sankey Marine, Worcester Road, Evesham; Tewkesbury Marina, Bredon Road, Tewkesbury.

Great Ouse (Norfolk): Priory Marina, Bedford; Buckden Marina, Buckden; Hartford Marina, Wyton; The Boathaven, St Ives; Westview Marina, High Street, Earith; Hermitage Marina, Earith; Ely Marina, Waterside, Ely.

Nene: Billing Aquadrome, Little Billing; Oundle Marina, Barnwell Road, Oundle.

Ouse (Yorkshire): Boroughbridge Marina, Boroughbridge; Naburn Marina, Naburn; Acaster Malbis.

Severn: Seaborne Yacht Co., Court Meadow, Kempsey; Upton Marina, East Waterside, Upton-on-Severn.

Thames: Val Wyatt Marine, Willow Lane, Wargrave; Racecourse Yacht Basin, Maidenhead Road, Windsor; Windsor Marina, Maidenhead Road, Windsor; Penton Hook Marina, Chertsey; Walton Marine Sales, Walton Bridge, Walton-on-Thames. Public slipways at Radcot, Bablock Hythe, Oxford, Wallingford, Reading, Mapledurham, Wargrave, Aston, Medmenham, Marlow, Cookham, Maidenhead, Weybridge, Walton-on-Thames, Kingston-upon-Thames, Teddington, Twickenham, Ham, Petersham, Isleworth, Chiswick, Mortlake, Barnes, Putney.

Trent: Shardlow Marina, Shardlow; Sawley Bridge Marina, Long Eaton; Nottingham Castle Marina, Castle Boulevard, Nottingham; Colwick Park Marina, Nottingham; Farndon Harbour Moorings Ltd, North End, Farndon; Newark Marina, 26 Farndon Road, Newark.

TRAILER LAUNCHING SITES (Contd.)

Canals

Birmingham Canal Navigations: M. E. Braine (Boatbuilders), Norton Canes.

Bridgewater: Lymm Marina, Lymm.

Calder & Hebble: Sowerby Marine, The Wharf, Sowerby; Aspley Basin.

Fossdyke & Witham: James Kendall & Co., Brayford Pool.

Grand Union: High Line Yachting, Iver; Denham Marina, 100 Acres, Denham; Cassio Bridge Marina, Watford; Willowbridge Enterprises, Stoke Road, Bletchley; Whilton Marine, Whilton Locks, Daventry; Stoke Locks, Stoke Bruerne; Braunston Marina, Braunston Junction; Foxton Boat Services, Bottom Lock, Market Harborough; Sileby Marina, Mountsorrel Lane, Sileby.

Lancaster: Nor'West Marina, Galgate.

Leeds & Liverpool: James Mayor & Co., Tarleton; White Bear Marina, Park Road, Chorley.

Llangollen: Black Prince Marina, Whixall.

Macclesfield: Macclesfield Marina, Brook Street, Macclesfield.

Oxford: Fenny Marine, Fenny Compton; Napton Marina, Stockton.

Peak Forest: New Mills Marina, Hibbert Street, New Mills.

Rochdale: Hebden Bridge Canal Basin.

Sheffield & South Yorks (Stainforth & Keadby): Staniland Ltd, Lock Hill, Thorne; Blue Water Marina Ltd, Thorne.

Shropshire Union: Barbridge Marina, Wardle; Venetian Marine, Cholmondeston.

Staffordshire & Worcestershire; Ashwood Marina, Kingswinford.

Trent & Mersey: Shobnall Marina, Burton-on-Trent; Stenson Marina, Stenson, Derby.

Worcester & Birmingham: Alvechurch Boat Centre, Scarfield Wharf, Alvechurch.

TRAILER LAUNCHING SITES (Contd.)

Lake District
Coniston Water: Coniston Boating Centre.

Derwentwater: Derwent Marina Watersports Centre, Portinscale.

Windermere: Windermere Aquatic Ltd, Glebe Road, Bowness-on-Windermere; Shepherd's Boatyard, Glebe Road, Bowness-on-Windermere; Ferry Nab, Bowness-on-Windermere; Waterhead Marine Ltd, Ambleside; Lowwood Hotel, Ambleside.

Norfolk Broads
River Ant: Richardsons (New Horizon) Ltd, Stalham; Stalham Yacht Services, Stalham.

Barton Broad: Cox Bros Boatyard, The Staithe, Barton Turf.

River Bure: The Street, Horning; Percival Boats Ltd, Ferry Corner, Horning.

Hickling Broad: Whispering Reeds Boatyard, Hickling.

Oulton Broad: Oulton Broad Yacht Station; Wherry Hotel; Colmans Land Slipway, Bridge Road.

River Thurne: Ludham Bridge Boat Service (Womack Water); Martham Boat Building Co.

River Waveney: Beccles Yacht Station; Burgh Castle Marina, Burgh Castle; Waveney Valley Boats, Puddingmoor, Beccles; Burgh St Peter; St Olaves.

River Yare: Brundall Marina, Riverside Estate, Brundall; Reedham Ferry Inn, Reedham Ferry.

Scotland
Caledonian Canal: Caley Cruisers, Inverness; Cameron Cruisers, Onich by Fort William; Highland Holiday Boats, Doch Garrock, Inverness.

Loch Lomond: Loch Lomond Marina, Balloch.

12

HIRING FOR CHOICE

When the canal system was first 'discovered' by pleasure boaters, superannuated 70-foot narrowboats could be picked up for the proverbial song. This happy situation lasted only as long as the supply outstripped the demand, and with the growing popularity of the waterways boat prices began to rise. Now a new full-length narrowboat might cost as much as £25,000, and even secondhand 30- or 40-footers are likely to carry price tags of five figures if they are in good condition.

With river cruisers the situation is much the same. Unless you start with a small and dilapidated cabin cruiser that you are prepared to work on, you will have to spend at the very least several thousands of pounds to get afloat. On top of the capital expenditure you will also have to find the money for certain standing costs – such as mooring fees, licence, insurance and maintenance – which will have to be paid whether you use the boat or not. And that's before you have gone anywhere.

To be frank, many boat owners are pouring money down the drain. With the pressure of work, the timing of holidays and the house and garden clamouring for attention, the time that can be spent afloat is strictly limited. The less use you get out of the boat, the more expensive it becomes. Take the following example as an illustration of this.

The standing fees outlined above might, in the case of a typical 30-foot river cruiser, easily come to £500 per year, on to which you have to add interest on the purchase price – even if you don't have to borrow the money, you will still be losing interest that your money would have earned in the building society – and depreciation. This might amount to £1,000 a year or more.

The minimum annual cost is therefore £1,500. If you then use the boat for only four weeks in the year – and many owners manage less than that – your boating will have cost you nearly £400 a week, not counting fuel or necessary repairs.

This is difficult to justify when you consider the alternative. There are literally thousands of hire craft available on Britain's rivers, canals and lakes, and a four-berth 30-foot river cruiser can be hired for under £300 a week even in the height of summer. You would need to be able to spend five weeks on your own boat to make ownership financially logical.

Nor is price the only reason for hiring. Once you have bought a boat, you are committed to that boat. You have to use it or sell it; you no longer have any choice of vessel. You are also committed in terms of where you cruise, since it will take the better part of a week to move it to another area only 100 miles away (unless it is a trailer boat – see Chapter 11).

Yet with hire craft there are no such constraints. If you have four weeks' holiday you can spend a week on the Thames, a week on the Norfolk Broads, a week on the narrow canals in the Midlands and a week on Lake Windermere if you wish. You can even go abroad and explore the magnificent Continental waterways such as the River Saône or the Canal du Midi in France, the Frisian Lake District of Holland or Denmark's Limfjord.

It would be fair to say that there are very few parts of Britain's waterways network that cannot be reached by hire craft. Every major canal and navigable river has at least one hire base, and in some areas, such as the Broads, there are literally dozens. How then to choose?

Hiring gives you the chance to use a boat you could never afford to buy – and to visit places it might take weeks to reach from your home mooring. These unusual diamond-shaped locks, incidentally, are on the Oxford Canal.

It was on the Broads that hire boating originated in the early years of this century. Two Broads-based campanies, Blakes and Hoseasons, now dominate the scene not only in East Anglia but nationally. Neither owns its own craft, but they act as booking agents for hire fleet operators throughout the country and abroad.

Both Blakes and Hoseasons produce thick colour brochures every year detailing the craft available for the coming season together with brief resumés of the areas in which they operate. If you have no preconceived idea of where you want to go, the brochures are a good place to start looking. Some examples of their 1986 prices are given in the panel below.

WHAT WILL IT COST?

As with any holiday, the cost of boat hire varies considerably with the season. The prices below are taken from hire companies' 1986 catalogues, and refer to three specific weeks: April 12–19, June 7–14 and August 2–9 (Saturday to Saturday; depending on individual operators' schedules, some may have different start days). Prices are inclusive of VAT and assume full occupancy; they may be lower if you do not use all the berths, or if some are taken up by young children. Bedding and use of gas is included; fuel is not, except where marked F, and neither is travel to and from the hire base.

Location and type of boat	Berths	Price in £		
		Apr	Jun	Aug
Broads, wide-beam cruiser	8	254	332	426
Grand Union Canal, narrowboat	10	278	384	480
North Holland, wide-beam cruiser	6	338	393	463
River Severn, wide-beam cruiser	5	233	310	398
River Shannon, wide-beam cruiser	4	200	290	350
Shropshire Union, narrowboat (F)	6	305	395	510

Needless to say, the choice of craft available extends beyond the list offered by the two agents. The British Waterways Board owns a sizeable hire fleet, and there are many other independent hire operators who advertise in newspaper small ads and in magazines such as *Waterways World* and *Canal & Riverboat*. Some operators have banded together in joint marketing ventures, the Blue Riband group being one of the more successful examples. A list of names and addresses appears in the Appendix to this book.

Rates vary appreciably according to season. During the off season of late September to late March you are likely to have to pay around half the price charged during the school summer holiday. Sometimes bargains are available when hirers have to cancel at the last minute, but there is no certainty of getting what you want and if you fail to book you may end up without a holiday at all.

Obviously the agents and operators would much prefer that you book early, since this helps spread their workload and helps them make projections for the coming year. It also ensures that they stay solvent, as the income from your deposit improves their cash flow. You might therefore be offered a discount for booking your holiday before the needles have dropped from the Christmas tree.

Many operators and agents protect themselves by saying that once the booking has been accepted and the deposit has been paid, the hirer is liable for the full balance even if he does not subsequently take the holiday. At the very least you are likely to lose your deposit should you cancel after this point, so if your plans are likely to change it pays to wait until they are confirmed even if this means you do not get the early booking discount.

For a premium of around £10 you can usually insure against an enforced cancellation, and indeed with some agents it is compulsory. Typically this pays the balance of the hire charge for you if you are 'forced to cancel prior to your holiday because of death, illness, injury, maternity, jury service, witness call, redundancy or unexpected Forces or occupational posting of you or any member of your party; or because of fire, storm, flood, subsidence or malicious damage rendering your home uninhabitable; or because of the police requiring your presence following a burglary at your home or place of business; or because of death or serious injury of a close relative or death of a business associate, partner or co-director'. All in all, a fairly comprehensive list.

The size of the initial booking deposit varies with the firm, and you may be asked to prepay for cancellation insurance and personal insurance. How far in advance you are expected to pay the balance of the hire charge also varies, but you are likely to have to cough up at least four and perhaps eight weeks before the start of the holiday.

Finally, you will be asked for a security deposit of as much as £100 on arrival at the boatyard. This may have to be paid in cash; check beforehand so that you do not have to hand over all your holiday spending money. The deposit will be refunded in full when you return the boat provided that it is undamaged and no gear is missing. As a rule, there are few operators who will charge for the odd broken glass or lost mooring spike, which they tend to accept as par for the course.

Fuel is usually, but not always, charged for separately. Where it is extra, the operator will fill the boat's tank for you at the start of the hire, measure how much is remaining at the end and charge you for the amount used. The money might be deducted from the security deposit, or you might be asked to pay a separate fuel deposit at the start.

If you do have to pay extra for fuel, the cost is unlikely to break the bank. As explained in Chapter 4, you can expect a consumption of around half a gallon per 10hp per hour with diesel, but this does not mean that a typical 70-foot narrowboat with a 20hp engine will be using a gallon an hour. Once the boat is travelling at the speed limit it needs very little power to keep going, so you should get away with an average consumption of under half a gallon an hour, or about 50p an hour at present prices.

Efficient firms will have anticipated most of the things you are likely to want to know, and will answer your questions either in the brochure or in an information pack sent out with the booking confirmation slip. It is worth studying the terms and conditions of hire in some detail to prevent misunderstandings.

This is particularly true of equipment. Nothing is more frustrating than taking over a boat on Friday night after the shops have shut to find that you cannot have a glass of wine with your supper because there is no corkscrew on board. If you are not given an inventory before the start of your holiday, ask for one.

It is a good idea to draw up a list of the items you consider essential and check them off against the inventory. Then you can make sure that anything that is not provided is brought from home. This is especially important in the case of the *batterie de cuisine*, where the operator's idea of a well-equipped galley may differ substantially from yours. All boats will have knives, forks, spoons, plates, cups, glasses, a few pans and other utensils; they are less likely to have, for example, sharp kitchen knives, a chopping board, a sieve, a pepper mill or a garlic press. Surprisingly, British hire boats are better in this respect than French ones, which never seem to have items as basic as mugs and a spatula.

Many operators will offer to do some shopping for you so that you do not have to carry a bootful of food from home. By all means take them up on the offer, but you should also take a supply of the household basics; there is no point in having 1lb of flour on board, for example, when you are only going to use a couple of ounces during the week. As suggested in Chapter 7, it is wise to decant small quantities of sugar, flour, herbs, spices and anything else that comes into this category into sealed containers at home and bring these along, together with the other galley essentials on your list.

Bedding is usually provided, but not necessarily towels. This will usually be made clear in the brochure or information pack. One common omission from the inventory is children's lifejackets; the boat will usually have lifejackets or buoyancy aids for as many adults as there are berths, but it is impractical to provide all the different children's sizes for all the boats in a hire fleet. Check beforehand to see what the operator has available.

Hire boats invariably have 12 or 24V electrics, so none of your household appliances will work on board. Low-voltage television sets are provided as an extra by most operators, but don't pin your hopes on being able to see your favourite programme. With the low aerial reception may be patchy, and the most attractive spot to moor for the night will not necessarily provide the best picture on the screen. If you cannot miss an episode of *EastEnders*, either record it on a video or stay at home.

Another extra worth considering is the hire of a bicycle or two. Not only will this make shopping easier when the nearest village is a couple of miles away, but it also will encourage you to explore more of the surrounding countryside. A bike is also useful when you are pushed to get back to the yard at the end of your holiday and are trying to make up time; one of the crew can cycle ahead along the towpath and get the locks ready for you.

If you are hiring a boat overseas, you will be offered a package deal that includes ferry or air travel. This is worth taking up even if you intend spending longer abroad than just the period of hire; the package rate will usually be substantially lower than the combined hire charge and normal fare.

One of the drawbacks of hiring a boat is that you have to return to the yard from which you started. Unless you are doing a 'ring' – a network of canals that brings you back to your starting point – this will mean that you have to turn round at the half-way stage and spend the second half of your holiday retracing your steps. But where an operator has two or more hire bases it may be possible to arrange a one-way cruise, leaving the boat at a different yard.

One particularly worthwhile example of this is on the Canal du Midi in southern France, where an easy fortnight's cruise on a Blue Line boat will take you from Marseillan to Castelnaudary (or Castelnaudary to Marseillan) and allow plenty of time for sightseeing. If you have a car, of

Oulton Broad, an ideal place for a first holiday afloat. Thousands of people have learnt to handle boats on the gentle waters of the Broads, and the boatyards are well versed in the art of instruction.

course, one of the crew will have to travel back to collect it, or you can arrange for someone from the boatyard to deliver it to the end base for you.

There are not many restrictions placed on hire craft, so it pays to make sure that you know what they are before departure. Among the more common are that you should not travel before dawn (as if anyone would on holiday!) or after sunset; that minors should not be left to steer the boat without adult supervision; and that you should not take an inland waterways cruiser on to coastal waters.

All operators will offer a free demonstration run, possibly up to and through the nearest lock, to give hirers a chance to familiarize themselves with the controls before being left in sole charge. The instructors are used to showing complete novices the ropes, and usually have a set presentation that assumes everyone is a novice until proved otherwise. Even if you are quite experienced it is worth going through the procedure as there may be points about the handling, for example, that are peculiar to that particular boat.

The demonstration run also serves another purpose in allowing the instructor to satisfy himself that his expensive boat is not being taken over by a lunatic. It is very rare for operators to refuse a booked charter, but they are quite entitled to – and required to by their insurers – if they suspect that you are incompetent. If the problem is simply that you have not mastered the controls, the instructor will usually extend the demonstration until you get it right, though you may be charged for the extra tuition.

Planning a route for your holiday is relatively easy; it is often a case of simply deciding whether to go up or down a canal or river. The operator will be able to tell you which offers the best cruising, and may have suggestions about where to moor up each evening. You should aim to get back to the hire base, or close to it, on the last night – no one wants to have to get up at five for a 10-mile dash back to the yard in order to hand the boat back at nine.

A guide to the waterways is invaluable, as it is otherwise all too easy to miss some of the sights which are not actually at the water's edge. At lunchtime, with tongues hanging out all over the boat, you can travel 10 miles without coming across a waterside pub, yet pass unsuspecting within 100 yards of half a dozen set back from the bank. One of the best of the many waterways guides available is the Nicholson's series, which include strip maps showing the position of shops, pubs, restaurants and places of interest.

You will also need a guide to tell you where the next water point is. Most hire craft have large enough fuel tanks to last you a week, but water is another matter, and you will almost certainly have to fill up *en route*. As a matter of course it is sensible to top up wherever possible rather than wait until the tank is nearly empty. If you know you have enough water to see you to the next but one water point, you can bet that the tap will be out of commission when you arrive. Life's like that.

Appendix
USEFUL CONTACTS

ASSOCIATIONS

The two associations most helpful to the boater are the Inland Waterways Association and the Royal Yachting Association. Both are umbrella organizations, and will be able to put you in touch with cruising clubs on individual waterways. The IWA also co-ordinates the work of restoration under its own Waterway Recovery Group.

Inland Waterways Association, 114 Regents Park Road, London NW1 8UQ. Tel: 01-586 2556.

Royal Yachting Association, Victoria Way, Woking, Surrey GU21 1EQ. Tel: 04862 5022.

MANAGING AUTHORITIES

The BWB manages 60 per cent of Britain's navigable waterways system, but there are many other authorities responsible for other parts of the network. A list of the areas they cover is given in Chapter 2.

Anglian Water Authority, Great Ouse Division, Clarendon Road, Cambridge. Tel: 0223 61561.

Associated British Ports, Kingston House Tower, Bond Street, Hull HU1 3ER. Tel: 0405 2691.

British Waterways Board, Melbury House, Melbury Terrace, London NW1 6JX. Tel: 01-262 6711.

British Waterways Board (Scotland), Caledonian Canal Office, Clachnaharry, Inverness. Tel: 0463 33140.

Conservators of River Cam, The Guildhall, Cambridge CB2 3QJ. Tel: 0223 58977.

Great Yarmouth Port & Haven Commissioners, 21 South Quay, Great Yarmouth. Tel: 0493 855151.

Hampshire County Council, The Castle, Winchester. Tel: 0962 4411.

Linton Lock Commissioners, Willow Garth, 10 Tentergate Lane, Knaresborough, Yorkshire.

Lower Avon Navigation Trust, Holloway, Pershore, Worcestershire WR10 1HW. Tel: 03865 2517.

Manchester Ship Canal Co., Estates Office, Dock Office, Trafford Road, Salford M52 2XB. Tel: 061-872 2411.

Middle Level Commissioners, March, Cambridgeshire. Tel: 03542 53232.

National Trust (Stratford-upon-Avon), Canal Office, Lapworth, Warwickshire. Tel: 05643 3370.

National Trust (River Wey), Dapdune Lea, Wharf Road, Guildford, Surrey. Tel: 0483 61389.

Ouse & Foss Navigation Trustees, Secretary, Town Clerk of York, Guildhall, York. Tel: 0904 54544.

Port of London Authority, London Dock House, Thomas More Street, London E1 9AZ. Tel: 01-481 4887.

Rochdale Canal Co., 75 Dale Street, Manchester M1 2HG. Tel: 061-236 2456.

South Lakeland District Council, PO Box 18, Stricklandgate House, Kendal, Cumbria LA9 4QQ. Tel: 0539 24007.

Surrey County Council, County Hall, Penrhyn Road, Kingston-upon-Thames, Surrey. Tel: 01-541 8911.

Thames Water Authority, Nugent House, Vastern Road, Reading RG1 8DB. Tel: 0734 593387.

Upper Avon Navigation Trust, Avon House, Harvington, Evesham, Worcestershire. Tel: 0386 870526.

Witham Fourth District Internal Drainage Board, 47 Norfolk Street, Boston, Lincolnshire. Tel: 0205 65226.

Yorkshire Water Authority, West Riding House, 67 Albion Street, Leeds LS1 5AA. Tel: 0532 448201.

BUYING A BOAT

The industry association is the British Marine Industries Federation. Both the BMIF and its affiliate, the National Yacht Harbours Association, a federation of marina operators, will help with general enquiries about boats and moorings. The Yacht Brokers, Designers and Surveyors Association can supply names and addresses of surveyors in your area.

National Yacht Harbours Association, Boating Industry House, Vale Road, Oatlands, Weybridge, Surrey KT13 9NS. Tel: 0932 54511.

British Marine Industries Federation, Boating Industry House, Vale Road, Oatlands, Weybridge, Surrey KT13 9NS. Tel: 0932 54511. General enquiries and free advice: 0932 45890.

Yacht Brokers, Designers and Surveyors Association, The Wheelhouse, 5 Station Road, Liphook, Surrey GU30 7DW. Tel: 0428 722322.

INSURANCE

Boat insurance is a specialized subject and, though many brokers will give you a quote, it pays to find someone with experience in inland waterways cover. These include:

Bradford Mays & Co., 16 Lower Guildford Road, Knaphill, Woking, Surrey. Tel: 04867 3277.

Desmond Cheers, 44 High Street, Hampton Hill, Middlesex. Tel: 01-977 8175.

The Boat Museum at Ellesmere Port.

The Navigators, Eagle Star House, 113 Queen's Road, Brighton, Sussex. Tel: 0273 29866.

O'Connor & Co. (Insurances) Ltd, 16 Billing Road, Northampton NN1 5AW. Tel: 0604 21747.

St Margarets Insurances Ltd, 153 High Street, London SE20 7DL. Tel: 01-778 0161.

Traffords Ltd, 151 Hatfield Road, St Albans, Hertfordshire. Tel: 0727 33241.

Andrew Weir Insurance Brokers Ltd (Marine Department), 17A/18 Bevis Marks, London EC3A 7BB. Tel: 01-283 1266.

FINANCE

As explained in Chapter 3, it pays to shop around for boat finance. Try your own bank, or even one with which you do not have an account, as well as the finance houses listed below.

Forward Trust Group, 12 Calthorpe Road, Edgbaston, Birmingham B15 1QZ. Tel: 021-454 6141.

Lombard North Central (Marine Finance Dept.), Freepost, Purley Way, Croydon CR9 9ER. Tel: 01-684 6911.

Mercantile Credit (Marine Finance Dept.), Freepost, Arundel Towers North, Portland Terrace, Southampton SO9 1BG. Tel: 0703 228775.

Security Pacific (Marine Finance Dept.), 308–314 Kings Road, Reading, Berkshire. Tel: 0734 61022.

HIRE AGENCIES AND OPERATORS

Apart from the agencies and groups given below, there are hundreds of small independent operators who advertise in the various boating magazines and are listed in the Brittain Publications/IWA annual *Inland Waterways Guide*.

Association of Pleasure Craft Operators, 35a High Street, Newport, Shropshire. Tel: 0952 831572.

Blakes Holidays Ltd, Wroxham, Norwich NR12 8DH. Tel: 06053 3221.

The Waterways Museum at Stoke Bruerne.

Blue Riband Group, Gailey Marine, The Wharf, Watling Street, Gailey, Staffordshire. Tel: 0902 790612.

Boat Enquiries Ltd, 41–43 Botley Road, Oxford OX2 0PT. Tel: 0865 727288.

British Waterways Leisure Hire, Cruiser Booking Office, Chester Road, Nantwich, Cheshire CW5 8LB. Tel: 0270 625122.

Hoseasons Boating Holidays, Sunway House, Lowestoft, Suffolk NR32 3LT. Tel: 0502 62211.

UK Waterways Holidays Ltd, Penn Place, Rickmansworth, Hertfordshire WD3 1EU. Tel: 0923 770040.

WATERWAYS MAGAZINES

Canal & Riverboat, A. E. Morgan Publications, Stanley House, 9 West Street, Epsom, Surrey KT18 7RL. Tel: 03727 41411.

Motor Boat & Yachting, Quadrant House, The Quadrant, Sutton, Surrey SM2 5AS. Tel: 01-661 3298.

Motor Cruiser, as *Canal & Riverboat*.

Waterways World, Kottingham House, Dale Street, Burton-on-Trent, Staffordshire. Tel: 0283 64290.

MAPS AND GUIDES

There are scores of books on individual waterways and cruising areas. The widest range of titles is available from the IWA and the mail order company Shepperton Swan. Imray's map of the network gives a general idea of how the inland waterways system is laid out. The Brittain/IWA guide contains brief details of and lists the services available on each waterway, but for a mile-by-mile guide to towns and villages along the banks the Nicholson's/Ordnance Survey series of guides is without peer. Edward's *Inland Waterways of Great Britain*, a huge tome, goes one better where details of the waterways themselves are concerned, but unlike the Nicholson guides does not list or show

the waterside facilities. *Where To Launch Your Boat* (referred to in Chapter 11) is available from Barnacle Marine.

Barnacle Marine, The Warehouse, Crowhurst Road, Colchester CO3 3JN. Tel: 0206 563726.

Inland Waterways Association, 114 Regents Park Road, London NW1 8UQ. Tel: 01-586 2556.

Shepperton Swan Ltd, 4 The Clock House, Upper Halliford, Shepperton, Middlesex TW17 8RU. Tel: 0932 783319.

MUSEUMS

Several museums specialize in the history of the waterways and are worth a visit whether you arrive by boat or by car.

The Black Country Museum, Tipton Road, Dudley, West Midlands. Tel: 021-557 9643.

The Boat Museum, Dockyard Road, Ellesmere Port, South Wirral. Tel: 051-355 1876.

Exeter Maritime Museum, The Quay, Exeter, Devon. Tel: 0392 58075.

Nottingham Canal Museum, Carrington Street, Nottingham. Tel: 0602 598835.

The Waterways Museum, Canalside, Stoke Bruerne, Northamptonshire. Tel: 0604 862229.

The Wharf, Llangollen, Clwyd, North Wales. Tel: 0978 860702.

MISCELLANEOUS

Queries about radio/TV frequencies (Chapter 7): BBC Engineering Information Dept, BBC, Broadcasting House, London W1A 1AA.

First Aid Manual and details of courses (Chapter 8) available from: British Red Cross Society, 9 Grosvenor Crescent, London SW1X 7EJ; St Andrew's Ambulance Association, St Andrew's House, Milton Street, Glasgow G4 0HR; St John Ambulance, 1 Grosvenor Crescent, London SW1X 7EF.

ACKNOWLEDGEMENTS

My thanks are due to Frances Moon and Alan Harper for their chapters on wildlife and architecture; to Alex McMullen and Ruth Baldwin, who picked the nits out of the manuscript; to Myrna White, who drew the diagrams; to my wife, Bim, for her support throughout; and to Anj, for her efforts on the final lap.

Most of the photographs were provided by Harry Arnold. Exceptions are the jacket photograph and those on pages 40, 59, 62, 71, 76, 116, 117, 119, 120, 167 and 169, from the archives of *Motor Boat & Yachting*; those in Chapter 9, taken by Kevin Carlson; and the picture of my own children on page 108.

INDEX